Personal Computers for Persons with Disabilities

Personal Computers for Persons with Disabilities

An Analysis, with Directories of Vendors and Organizations

William Roth

McFarland & Company, Inc., Publishers
Jefferson, North Carolina, and London

I would like to thank the Disability Solutions Group of
Apple Computer, Inc., and the HEATH Resource Center
of the American Council on Education, for permission to
include material from lists of theirs. I am also grateful for
other material reprinted with permission from Assistive
Technology Sourcebook, RESNA Press, copyright © 1990
RESNA. Special thanks is given to Apple Computer, Inc.,
for permission from DLM to reproduce the organization
section of *Apple Computer Resources in Special Education and
Rehabilitation,* copyright ©1988, 1989, 1990. I would also like
to acknowledge the invaluable assistance of Carol Cohen,
Alexandra Enders, Lori Hansel, and Gary Moulton.

British Library Cataloguing-in-Publication data are available

Library of Congress Cataloguing-in-Publication Data

Roth, William, 1942–
    Personal computers for persons with disabilities : an analysis,
with directories of vendors and organizations / by William Roth.
        p.   cm.
    Includes bibliographical references and index.
    ISBN 0-89950-698-4 (sewn softcover : 50# alk. paper) ∞
    1. Computers and the handicapped.   2. Computerized self-help
devices for the handicapped.   3. Microcomputers.   4. Computers and
the handicapped—United States—Directories.   5. Microcomputers—
United States—Directories.   6. Computerized self-help devices for
the handicapped—United States—Directories.   I. Title.
HV1569.5.R67   1992
362.4'0483—dc20   91-50944
                                                                          CIP

Manufactured in the United States of America

*McFarland & Company, Inc., Publishers
  Box 611, Jefferson, North Carolina 28640*

For Daniel Roth, with respect and love.

Table of Contents

Preface

In 1983, I set out to do a book on public policy and art. I believe then and I do now that this is a significant issue into which I had some insight. The project progressed rapidly. The first and easiest insight was the numerous ways that our government supports the arts. Even now I get carried away.

I have a disability that makes it almost impossible for me to type effectively. Further, this disability makes it difficult for me to create, organize, and retrieve notes. I had worked around and through such problems in the past. I had also become a bit familiar with computers and used them slightly for econometric and factor analysis. I knew that they had large memories and could perform simple operations quickly. Perhaps they were the answer to some problems.

I asked my research assistant to enter my notes, preliminary drafts, and promising quotations on my project, the arts and public policy, onto the University's mainframe computer, not knowing exactly what I would do with them. As matters turned out, they were left incomplete. A book, perhaps a good book, remains unwritten.

From activity in the disability rights movement, I knew people and organizations to contact about the uses of computers for people with disabilities. I found two things. There was, even then, technology to do the jobs that I needed done and more. However, people with disabilities were not using this technology. I knew enough about technology to reckon this a waste and enough about people with disabilities to reckon this waste unnecessary and hence tragic.

I teach at the University at Albany, State University of New York, in the School of Social Welfare. I thank them for what happened next. In 1984 I established the Center for Computing and Disability, and they provided resources to give the Center a chance.

It was a gamble on all our parts. I mapped out in my mind a vision of the Center that was close to what it has become. I did not want the Center to focus narrowly on students with disabilities at one university. I wanted the Center to be a model for others, to broadcast its activities, to be a pulpit, to contribute to the debate on technology and disability in public policy, to provide the sort of social entrepreneurship that was lacking... In short, I did not want to spend time establishing a Center that was anything short of excellent and significant.

My university bought the idea. It is my satisfaction that they have been repaid. It is a greater satisfaction that what started as a substantially private vision shared by me and a few others throughout the country is now shared by many.

At the beginning came the task of raising funds. Whether money or vision is more important may be an interesting question, but I did not have time for it. I formed the New York State Council for Technology and Disability.

In 1985 and the beginning of 1986 efforts were succeeding on several fronts. Governor Mario M. Cuomo put the State of New York behind the Center and, more importantly, behind technology and disability. He and his excellent staff have my thanks for believing in a project when few did. The next year the Governor created a task force on technology and disability that created a document that in many ways was visionary. Its recommendations were implemented.

The State University of New York continued and augmented its generous support by way of enthusiasm, cash, and in-kind contributions. Without their nourishment and support the Center would surely have been impossible.

In 1986 John Akers, chairman of the board of IBM, was kind enough to lend a full time executive to the Center for Computing and Disability.

In 1985 I submitted a proposal to the United States Office of Special Education, Post-Secondary Division, to fund a model project. In 1986, I was pleasantly surprised to receive notice that the project had been funded.

The federal, state, university and corporate endorsements were invaluable not only in providing funding streams to realize the Center but in the recognition of the Center's promise and the significance of people with disabilities. My gratitude, acknowledgment, and debt to all these sources of support, especially my university, will forever be beyond my capacity to repay. Regard this book as a thank you note. Repayment, however, is within the capacity of people with disabilities using modern computing technology, and they have already done so.

My acknowledgments also extend to the people whom I have had the pleasure of knowing most directly in connection with the Center for Computing and Disability. These include the people with disabilities whom the Center has matched with appropriate computing technology, the cohorts of students who have passed through the Center's classes on computing and disability, my many superb colleagues at the Center, a supportive university administration, and help and encouragement from many across the State and Nation. I am overwhelmed and humbled.

To my former student and colleague now working with computers and disability, Bruce Bailey, I owe incalculable thanks for adding his wisdom to this book while a manuscript.

To my family, I am grateful, not only for their patience in my writing of this book, but also for their doubly patient part in the realization of my dream — the Center, long well established and stable.

The people at the Center and University have names. It is appropriate that I mention a few: Mary Ann Burke, Merideth Butler, Carol Connoly, Jean Delassandro, Mario Fario, Rachelle Fontek, Jean Gullahorn, Lori Hansel, Francis Lees, Warren Ilchman, Bruce Johnstone, Richard Read, Anita Rothschild, Gichou Shen, John Shumacher, Lynn Videka-Sherman, Fran Stevens. Thank you and others.

Necessary pain is unfortunate;
unnecessary pain is an abomination.

Enabling

Computing, a technology developed for all, promises enormous benefits to people with disabilities. New technologies and computing in particular, coupled with social change, harbor a significant promise. This promise is to alter disability by changing the technological and social environments so as to make them accessible to people with disabilities.

Although the new technologies (brought to mind by terms like "hitech," "computer," "space age," and "silicon") are not specifically designed for people with disabilities, they allow these people to interact with the world, with or through them, with an ease once unimaginable.

The new technologies, and the personal computers that are part of some and a portal into many, may well suggest a restructuring of our conception of disability. Their flexibility suggests that disability is not an intrinsic property of a person. Rather, the new technologies suggest defining disability in relation to the technologies. We can imagine established notions of impairment giving way to notions of interaction with new technologies.

Disability may be thought of in terms of input or throughput or output. People with sensory disabilities may have problems with the output of the new technologies; people with motor disabilities may have problems with input. Those with cognitive and mental disabilities insofar as such disabilities can be thought of in terms of a computer, can be said to have throughput disabilities. Of course, there are multiple disabilities and even where these do not exist, input, throughput, and output cannot be cleanly separated for all people. Nonetheless, these notions constitute an inkling of a new idea of functional impairment.

In the future it seems possible that modifications and improvements in new technologies will change the nature of input, throughput and output disabilities, rendering even those categories of disability irrelevant.

1

What must be done so as to not lose several generations of people with disabilities and to turn into reality future possibilities for people with disabilities? In the present work we deal with what exists, specifically personal computers, and what can be done with them.

With the current state of technology, most people with disabilities are not technologically disabled or computer disabled as they have no particular inherent difficulty with technology. Nonetheless, these people are or can be profoundly affected by the new technologies. They point to what these new technologies can do for people with disabilities in general and by doing so suggest the importance of connecting disabled people with appropriate technologies and personal computers in particular.

For example, a person who rides a wheelchair instead of walking may well have no computer disability. Yet usually such people are thought of as disabled. Traditional architecture can be modified. Still, problems remain. It may be difficult to reach the top drawer of a file cabinet, to make a trip to retrieve data, to do any of the things that legs may do better than wheels. Yet insofar as the wheelchair rider interacts with the new electronic architectures, what used to be an impairment is irrelevant. These architectures do not discriminate between wheelchair riders and users of shoe leather.

As the wheelchair rider relates to others and to other environments through these electronic architectures, interactions in such environments will be nondisabling as well. For example, suppose that the wheelchair rider is a lawyer. If it is difficult to do legal research from a wheelchair, case law can be found on a database called WestLaw. What the wheelchair riding lawyer needs is a computer that can access WestLaw.

The new technologies, coupled with social change, harbor a significant promise. The impaired person with no problem of input, throughput, or output can benefit dramatically from new technologies, because new environments are increasingly for everyone and because new environments serve as a substitute for old environments and as a mediation between the person and the environment. By making the wheelchair rider nondisabled on the job, new architectures will render her or him less disabled elsewhere by virtue of the salary that accompanies a job and the self-esteem that goes with a job well done.

What is true for the wheelchair rider holds for the elderly person who has trouble walking, the person with a heart condition, or any of a variety of people. While situations like these may have been disabling with older technologies, they need not be so with the new. A priority is to make new technologies available to those requiring only the usual education in their use, but who stand to benefit disproportionately from them. But these technologies benefit other persons with disabilities.

Currently, the way that many people interface with electronic architecture is through a personal computer keyboard that looks much like the average typewriter keyboard. But a typewriter keyboard is not the only way to input symbols. The use of the keyboard is from habit. Personal computers and other digital electronic technologies recognize only strings of "0's" and "1's"—binary code. In fact, symbols on the keyboard are translated into such code.

Just about anybody can produce binary code, just by manipulating an on-off switch. Moving an eyebrow, bopping a switch with a foot or head, or puffing or sipping, are a few of the manifold ways of producing binary code. Electromyograph and electroencephalogram potentials are ways of getting binary code. There are so many ways to produce binary code that motor disability of almost any sort is an insufficient obstacle to code production and therefore to accessing many electronic technologies and modern computers. The binary workings signal the possibilities for people with disabilities.

Further means of computer input, designed to make the computer accessible to all, make it more accessible to many people with disabilities. For example, the pen is emerging as an alternative to the keyboard. No longer will it be necessary to type in order to use a computer. Voice input is another burgeoning alternative to the keyboard. No longer will it be necessary to use hands and fingers in order to operate a computer. Such technologies and others make the personal computer more accessible to more people with disabilities opening an electronic portal onto the worlds of work, play, and independent living. By so doing they increase accessibility to the social and technological worlds.

Even in the hands of a skilled operator, binary code can only be produced slowly. This led to some economies in the wording of telegrams. This "telegraph style" took avantage of redundancy in ordinary language. While this may be acceptable for some purposes (such as taking notes on a notebook computer), usually it is neither acceptable nor sufficient.

Yet, there are methods for the computer operator to overcome the difficulty of slow input. Mathematics is a parsimonious language, as are most computer programming languages. Certain programming languages, such as APL, are even stingier and of potential use for some with disabilities. What is true of mathematics and programming is true for many other applications as well.

Word processing offers vast advantages over writing for almost anyone. With it, it is easier, quicker, and simpler to produce a document. Word processing is better for the able-bodied person than typing. Packages exist that produce shorthand (i.e., *PRD +*), anticipate probable words (i.e., *MindReader*), type appropriate macros (the macro for this might be "TAP"), and otherwise expand input (*QuicKey* developed at the Trace Research and Development Center is designed for disability; others are not but are useful for people with disabilities). A list of products mentioned here—how much, who makes them, where, and more—is found in Appendix A.

We can expect further improvements. Some of these will be disability-oriented, but most will not. A principle that has already emerged from computing technology is that what is good for everybody is likely to be good for people with disabilities. A prime example of this is the modern, inexpensive personal computer that integrates (or mainstreams) people with disabilities to live and work alongside their able-bodied peers.

Through binary code almost anybody can interact with computers. Although interaction may be eased by appropriate hardware and software, it may still be slow. Still, there are many ways to increase speed.

Symbols like the alphabet can scan on the screen and a "yes" decision can be sent once the proper symbol is designated. Switches can increase a "yes/no" binary choice by two to various powers. For example, a joystick increases it, a fire button increases the choices by another factor of two. The keyboard, the usual mode of input, can be regarded as a collection of switches. (Their arrangement as a keyboard is unnecessary and can be approximated by various other switching systems.)

Although there are substitutes for keyboards, they are often unnecessary. Many people with disabilities can use keyboards, especially with the features of a microcomputer, such as the BACKSPACE/ DELETE key that can reduce the consequences of error. A person with a disability is likely to share with others a trade-off of speed versus accuracy. The BACKSPACE/DELETE key is one of many features that enhances this trade-off.

Many people with disabilities may wish to press the SHIFT/CONTROL/ALT keys in series, rather than simultaneously with other keys. *ProKey* and *SuperKey* allow this as one option, Trace R&D Center has developed another package, and others exist.

For some people it might be useful to rearrange the keyboard. *ProKey* and *SuperKey* allow this. It might be important to move the cursor more quickly and accurately. *Cruise Control* and *Repeat Performance* allow this. For others it might be necessary to keep a diary, notes, appointment book, telephone dialer, and more; *SideKick II* and many other packages allow this.

In general people with disabilities are beneficiaries of the move to improve computers. The solutions will not isolate people with disabilities, but will integrate them under the new architecture.

The appropriate computing interface will often require ingenuity, trials, and error. Keep some general principles in mind:

One. Do not depart from the standard unless there is good reason. Know about existing peripherals and software for able-bodied persons. What is expensive today will be inexpensive tomorrow; therefore, be prudent in making expensive investments.

Two. A personal computer should produce output in a most standard manner.

Three. Unless otherwise strongly indicated, equipment should have open architecture and be constructed in modular fashion, allowing for the future addition of modifications not yet needed or not yet existent.

Four. If possible, modifications should be transparent to standard software and hardware: computers should run without "knowing" that the modification is in place.

Five. Low-tech solutions or no-tech common sense solutions should not be forsaken for hi-tech glamour. For example, a mouthstick, head-pointer, or keyguard may be invaluable.

Much more exists, including the following:

Several devices use head motion in a more elaborate and more efficient manner than a mouth or head stick. These all involve pointing the head at a set of symbols. The symbols selected are inputted.

Several devices recognize eye movement; there are more subtle ones in research laboratories. Often unaffected by motor disabilities, eye movement has substantial promise.

The mouse is practical although, unfortunately, it is often unusable by many with disabilities. Other peripherals have mouse emulation. Track balls (which can be operated by a foot), joysticks, touch screens, and digitizing pads are promising. The solutions to disabilities and computing are diverse and changing.

Voice input is seductive if not generally optimal. At the low end are a myriad of products that recognize the letters of the alphabet and some other symbols. Symbols can be strung together to represent words, words to form sentences, sentences to form paragraphs, etc. At the high end are input alternatives including IBM's *VoiceType, Dragon Dictate,* and others. They work, they are not toys. In the future such technology will be yet better.

Dramatic decreases in memory costs have been achieved. Inexpensive hard disks remove the burden of inserting floppies and allow for accessible files. More is becoming possible, from dialing a phone to making an airline reservation, to placing a stock order, to retrieving data, to corresponding with others, to being a draftsperson without being able to hold a pencil. Personal computers promise a full contributing life to many persons with a disability.

Computers can make physical architectures more accessible to many people with disabilities. A library of the future put on media like CD-ROM would be accessible by computer terminals anywhere, anytime.

More of the physical environment is accessible as well. For example, appliances in residences can be controlled by personal computers. In principle, offices can be controlled, and production lines can be operated by computer robotics. Much is possible. Significantly more would be possible with only marginal modifications for people with disabilities.

In the future the environment will be so changed that our idea of disability will change. As New York State Governor Mario M. Cuomo stated in his 1986 State of the State message, "One way to alter attitudes about disabilities and simultaneously to help people with disabilities realize their full potential is to see that they have access to the complete array of society's technological advances. For many persons with physical and developmental disabilities, the year 2000 has already arrived. The computer, for example, has a special service to do for persons with disabilities, and its applications are beginning to become known to people who are blind, visually impaired, deaf and hearing impaired. The pace of technological change in this field outstrips the organizational, social and entrepreneurial modifications required to bring these powerful tools to people with disabilities."

I will conclude this chapter with an example of what is possible for people with disabilities. Consider John (since he is our creation we can call him by his first name). As it happens, he is an academic.

Like many professors, John has a measure of control over his life, although this is limited at times by his institution and at times by the interface of his disability with his work life. Much of this disabling interface is caused by the actions and attitudes of people in John's world. This is usually not the result of malice, bigotry, or hostility, but the result of ignorance and a misinterpretation of John's situation.

In some measure these obstacles result from the way John works. John rides a wheelchair, a technology that replaces the way other people relate to their surroundings when they walk. The wheelchair's usefulness has been enhanced by curb cuts, electric doors, ramps, and elevators. These accommodations are useful for many others. Bicycle riders use the curb cuts, as do people pushing baby carriages. The ramp to the school auditorium is used by one out of two people, and John has wondered why.

John's hands do not always do as he intends. For example, John was unable to maintain a neat desk, so he often resorted to memory. Still, his brain was too overburdened to immediately identify the location of papers on his sloppy desk. This situation led some of his colleagues to think him a slob. John's messy typing was also a drawback, although the pithiness of his letters to the editor made him a star in the local newspaper.

However, his life has changed dramatically with computers. John has many interests, ranging from Shakespeare to baseball. One day the Dean walked by John's office and noticed that it was a model of neatness, with a personal computer displayed prominently on his desk.

John has a filing system for his baseball facts on the hard disk of his computer. Another program allows him to keep a calendar, so that he no longer misses meetings. John also uses a telephone dialer and a software program that allows him to enter information one key at a time. With his modem he can communicate with other Shakespeare and baseball fans and with a library.

John had problems with libraries. Even when an elevator was installed in the library, he was unable to go through the stacks and had trouble with the card catalog. The library now has an electronic card catalog, and the works of Shakespeare are on CD-ROM at John's university.

Accessible to John's personal computer, the computer Shakespeare allows for all kinds of searches. This morning John had a question about when a king appears first and last in a certain Shakespearean play. When he arrived at his office, John could check out this esoteric insight through a computer.

John has developed other techie habits. Accompanying him in his wheelchair is a notebook computer that he uses to take notes everywhere. Since he is an insomniac, this computer is by the side of his bed in case he wants to write poetry in the early hours of the morning. It is simple to transfer what is on his notebook onto his personal computer. John also handles his own financial planning, finding direct access to various investment services valuable.

John's world has changed with computers. The worlds of most people with disabilities are worlds of the past. If people with disabilities are excluded from the new electronic architectures an opportunity will have been lost to more fully integrate them into society. The time to include them is now.

Electronic architectures and computers are here, but sufficient answers to how human beings deal with them are not. The interface between them is one of the grand challenges for human beings.

It is appropriate we should have coined the term "user-friendly" for computers. Insofar as human beings are forced into unfriendly architectures, a past injustice will be continued. It is hardly surprising that the problem of interfacing with electronic architectures is shared by people who are disabled. The concept "user friendly" situates the problem correctly, and helps make it amenable to solution for able-bodied and disabled users alike.

Just as the industry is trying to make its products "user friendly" for market reasons, so should this industry pay attention to the many Americans who have disabilities. The next generation may not call them disabled, for, properly constructed, the new architectures will interface with everyone. What earlier generations regarded as problems, a new generation will consider challenges.

Matching

It may have occurred to some readers with disabilities that they might want a personal computer. If the reader is a parent or a professional working with people with disabilities a similar thought may have crossed the mind. If so, which personal computer?

This question may be of interest to other readers as well. I hope to provide an answer by providing examples of how I match people with disabilities with appropriate computing technology. The reader can translate much of this into her or his purpose.

I speak of a match because that seems most adequately to denote the endeavor. To call it a prescription would be needlessly pretentious and medical; authorization seems too bureaucratic; evaluation is too broad. Match will do just fine.

The Center for Computing and Disability at the University of Albany, among other things, matches people with disabilities with appropriate computing technology. Making these matches is surely one of the most enjoyable things that I do. This is not because I am a bleeding heart do-gooder; but because of the thrill that comes with the application of knowledge to achieve a significant purpose for the person with the disability who is often unaware of what computers can do.

As example, a man some two years graduated from his encounter with cancer came for a match. Cancer connotes death, and we do not usually anticipate the disability that may be left in its wake or the wake of its treatment. Buck (such will be his pseudonym) had an oral cancer. Typically, this had been treated with surgery and radiation. In Buck's case, a consequence of the treatment was that he could no longer speak.

The session started, as they usually do, with my asking seemingly irrelevant questions, which, however, soon elicited a profile of Buck's intelligence, literacy, inner strength, and knowledge of computers.

Usually people come along with the person with a disability. I address my questions to the person with the disability. It is important that these sessions be a chapter in the respect and dignity of the person with the disability. Further, a person spoken to is more likely to answer. Buck brought company.

Buck—he allowed me to call him by his first name—communicated with a stenographer's pad and pencil, writing short pungent answers, turning the pad around so that I could see it. After I had read the answer, the pad was turned back, the previous comments slashed out in preparation for the next round in our discussion. I thought I knew what the answer to the next question would be.

Bill: "Do you type?"

Buck: "Yes."

Bill: "About how fast?"

Buck: "55 words per minute."

Bill: "On a typewriter?"

Buck: "An electric typewriter."

Bill: "You will be able to go faster on a word processor. We have one here that talks. Do you want to try it?"

Scene two found Buck at the keyboard of a word processor that, with an appropriate combination of hardware and software, pronounced words as he typed. Buck's comments, questions, and answers lengthened. He smiled. Our communication became easier.

About ten minutes later I asked Buck how he liked the talking computer. Buck's one word answer was "Fantastic!"

We have one happy and excited man. His energy mobilized around using a computer to do something important to him, it will be used throughout the rest of the session.

Lesson I: Get the person on the computer as soon as possible.

Lesson II: Get the person involved with something of genuine interest. Excitement is a good introduction to learning.

Lesson III: Do not take conventional labels, diagnoses, or assessments too seriously. Even when accurate in their own right, they are usually of limited relevance in using the computer.

Lesson IV: Observe as closely as you listen. Information not used immediately should be filed away for possible future action. Dissonances between observation and words should be thought about.

Lesson V: Do not short sell the person. This is tricky. Disabled people go through too much of their lives not being taken seriously. There are special circumstances here. For example, the person with the disability may not know what a computer can do and what he or she can do with a computer. The person with the disability may have little self confidence or may be trained in habits of despair and dependence.

The session ended with agreement and enthusiasm by the person with the disability. This ending qualifies as Lesson VI.

As I talked with Buck it became clear that he was smart. I raised the possibility of employment at home, explaining why he might want it and why he might not. Buck said he would rather work at home. He said it rather quickly. I asked why.

Lesson VII: Whenever a person with disability makes a major decision regarding the future, be prepared to question it. It may be made based on poor information or a questionable proclivity. Particularly when a person undercuts her or his abilities is a question in order.

Buck said that he thought others might have a hard time accepting him. I asked if he wanted to hear my opinion, and he answered, "Yes." I submitted that his bandages were among the least stigma, that talking with a computer might be seen as a novelty, while having a tilted head might cause problems. Buck said that he still would like to work at home. I provided the modem and communication software to facilitate it.

Lesson VIII: Answer questions honestly and do not be afraid to raise questions. Yet never forget that matching sessions are not psychotherapy. If psychological issues do arise, be certain they are dealt with by the end of the session.

These lessons are among the many lessons that I have learned from people with disabilities. This is Lesson IX: Be open to learning as much as you can from people with the disabilities. This is not only because the person with the disability is often a world class expert on her or himself, but also because the person's wisdom, insight, and imagination can be brought to bear on the match.

To close (or perhaps open) the book on Buck, I matched him with a portable computer with a quality voice that did not sound like Hal in *2001*. The computer was portable because voices are. Since portables do not like to be dropped, I asked Buck to carry one along for several minutes.

Buck was matched with appropriate adaptive software, a popular word processor, and a popular spreadsheet. Further, he was matched with a modem in case he did want to work at home as well as with a letter quality dot matrix printer. Finally, all the software was installed to load in proper sequence from a hard disk with a menuing system to protect Buck from the operating system unless he wanted to become familiar with it.

The process of fitting a computer with software is called configuring. It is important, particularly for computer novices, that configuring be done correctly, lest the user take upon him or herself responsibility for mistakes that are in reality mistakes of the computer.

Lesson X: Make access to the personal computer as easy as possible, "user friendly." This is the reason for the hard disk that makes loading programs into the computer easier for everyone and possible for some people with disabilities. It is also a reason for a menuing or graphic system, where the user sees a menu or icons on the computer screen and selects the desired program from the screen.

The session made for an easy match with a profound difference for Buck's life. It is true of almost everyone who is disabled that they stand to benefit from being matched with an appropriate personal computer. Further, the clarity of Buck's match is replicated surprisingly often.

Match the person with the disability with the least expensive equipment that will truly do the job now and in the immediate future. And computing technology changes quickly; it is imprudent to provide for far off future scenarios.

Yet even appropriateness now mandates that many economies are false. People with disabilities put up with second best too often. Providing the second best in computing technology is a favor to no one. On the other hand providing color postscript laser printers and 80486 50 megahertz CPU based computers is usually gratuitous. It is neither too cheap nor too dear. This delicate curve must guide matches.

If the person with a disability is paying, he or she may forego the élan of a Ferrari for the economy of four cylinders. Yet a heap is not in order either in cars or computers. If a third party like the school system or the vocational rehabilitation system is paying, recognize that they act as proxies for the tax payer. Further, providing cost effective solutions is the best way to earn a reputation for honesty that leads to the acceptance of matches by the third party payer.

A youth named Skip bounced by one day. He had no difficulty operating computers. He fell into that catch-all basket "learning disabled." But Skip appeared to have genuine difficulties in writing. As it turned out, he was incompetent in math as well. Skip explained that his teachers, knowing how important writing was, had spent all their time teaching him how to write and none in teaching him other things.

Personal computers were of modest help in his writing. To be so they had to be integrated into his school environment. His math skills were perhaps too easy to fix to ever be attended to.

Lesson XI: The successful use of personal computers by students with disabilities mandates a change in the organization of the schools. This could be greeted as a challenge or as a burden. If the latter happens, a great opportunity will have been lost as well as another generation of students with disabilities. This is all the more sad because the work place is changing rapidly to make it more accessible to people with disabilities, less accessible to the many failures, disabled and able bodied, of some conventional educational practice.

A young woman with cerebral palsy rode in one day. Lesson XII: Almost invariably the medical or pseudomedical character of disability is irrelevant. We are interested in the way a person interacts with a personal computer, with input, output, and throughput disabilities. Often medical status degenerates outside of the clinic into mere or even harmful labels.

A match with the personal computer is meant to last for a time. Changes in the nature of the disability may well have an effect on the match. Insofar as the medical label is a guide to such changes, it may be useful. Usually, questions regarding change are answered accurately and easily by the person with the disability.

We talked a while. This young woman, Monica, rolled up to a computer. I called for my best guess of appropriate software: A software package named *Filch* that controls for many motor difficulties, one called *MindReader* that speeds up input, and *Turbo Lightning* that checks for spelling errors or typos as they occur. Although it is theoretically possible to proceed deductively from a person's impairments, goals, tasks, and environment, I have found it altogether more accurate to have an array of equipment at hand in the room to try out as a match with the person.

Monica was sent with the expectation that she learn to become a word processor. Despite the advantages of word processing over typing, the input required to do a job is still greater than with most applications of a computer. It turned out that Monica was bright, and that word processing would be a relatively weak entry into the job market for her.

Perhaps young women are thought of as secretaries. I asked Monica what she would like to do forgetting about her disability. It turned out that she wanted to be an accountant, and we discussed the computer nature of modern accounting. Lesson XIII: Do not stereotype nor sell short.

It became clear that Monica was college material. A college degree enhances employment prospects and otherwise contributes to the quality of life. Lesson XIV: Bear in mind the appropriateness of further education and the role of the personal computer in furthering education.

An invaluable use of these sessions is to open new horizons made possible by a personal computer. In so doing, it is valuable to have as many concerned people as possible at the session. Their witness to the promise of computing, their potential advocacy, is invaluable for the person with the disability. Lesson XV: Invite along as many people as possible to the matching session.

Each session has its own drama, but we offer the following guidelines to keep in mind when matching a computing system with a person with a disability.

1. Bear in mind the tasks to be done as well as possible future tasks and be sure that the hardware, software, and peripherals that you select are appropriate to do the tasks.

The personal computer is an investment. Its cost must be measured against benefits both tangible and intangible. Therefore, while perhaps the easy system for currently projected and future use might be a super elaborate system, that often is not a cost effective solution. Be judicious.

2. Do not wait.

Yet you should not wait for a new machine before matching except in special circumstances. New hardware and software has a way of not appearing at all, "vaporware" goes the jargon, or of appearing much later than thought.

3. Choose, if possible, software and hardware that is standard.

You might be surprised at how far you can go with a standard computer. The reasons to remain standard are to simplify maintenance, to enhance learning, and to allow for future growth in the system. Standard and best do not always go together. The most popular data based management system is not universally the best, the most popular spreadsheet is not always the best, and some good word processors do not have substantial market share. But it is important to select software that is common because often additions to software or additions to standard packages evolve through time. Also others are likely to use common hardware and software.

The environment where one works is likely to depend on standard software and hardware. Of course, where adaptive software and hardware is necessary, you may have to give up standardization.

4. Consider the nonobvious. Maybe a person with a disability ought to have a notebook computer, a color monitor, a modem, or any of a number of devices that are more or less standard but may not be immediately thought of as of first-order importance.

Disability

To talk about disability without contexts that include society, people, organizations, money, politics and so on would be to talk about an abstraction. It is only in relation to these contexts that disability emerges as what it is. Disability cannot be understood without close relationship to context. Thus, an understanding of disability necessarily involves thinking about relationships to contexts that at first blush appear to extend beyond disability.

People with disabilities encounter the contexts of many different social systems, the definition of disability often varying according to the system. For example, a disabled child seeing a pediatrician for her or his disability is diagnosed in terms of chronic illness. In school, the definition of disability is different, and the teacher's definition may or may not jibe with that given by the pediatrician. As the child grows into an adult, perhaps in a transition into vocational rehabilitation, definitions change again.

Bureaucracies may have their own definitions for their own reasons. Whether these reasons are for the benefit of the person with disabilities or for the benefit of the bureaucracy is another question.

Our ordinary conceptions of disability are strange. We seem absolutely sure of the application of terms like "handicapped" or "disabled." Upon probing, black and white distinctions turn into grays. For example, what degree and what kind of visual impairment is required before we refer to an individual as blind? Do eyeglasses constitute a disability, or are they a technological response to a disability, or do they show a preference over contact lenses? Sureness is grounded in quicksand.

Disability is expressive of a relationship between a person and environment as refracted through society. If society perceives the relationship to be askew, mismatched, or troublesome, the relationship constitutes a disability.

Disability arises from an interaction between a person and the environment. Computers, an interface of the person and the environment, have an effect on the interaction. Computers can aid in enabling environments to a degree generally not feasible in the past. Their power comes from how they can change the interaction.

At an early stage in our development as a species, we lived in a world not of our own making. It was a world of nature, by some accounts a hostile world, largely outside the control of people. The history of the species has been one of the construction of environments by people to augment and even replace natural environments.

The environments of today are largely fashioned by people, not fact but artifact. This changes disability. It is one thing for disability to express a relationship to a natural environment, another thing for disability to express a relationship to an environment fashioned by people. In a natural environment (state of nature), disability resided often within the person who was disabled and in relationships as with family, friend, and neighbor. Any attempt to modify the environment was either doomed to failure, or, where successful, the environment became that much more fashioned by people. Perhaps too many people, too frequently, found themselves disabled before the power of nature. Arguably, this is a reason that environments have become ever more fashioned by people.

Disability only exists as refracted through society. Imagine what a primitive society might have conceived disability to be. Disability would have looked different from today.

Disability has its share of literary classics. Among these is a small book by Nora Groce, *They All Spoke Sign Language: Hereditary Deafness on Martha's Vineyard.* This elegant jewel is about settlers on Martha's Vineyard who carried a recessive gene for deafness. Deafness occurred without regard to social position, gender or other characteristics and, as the laws of heredity were then unknown, mysteriously.

The randomness and inevitability of occurrence led to an interesting social adaptation. Everyone learned sign language. This sign language was a creation of Martha's Vineyard and nonderivative of any standard sign language. It was not only spoken, people dreamed in it. A few of Groce's informants, remembering the old days, signed unconsciously as they talked.

There were no telephones, and so sign language proved useful for communicating across long distances and in noisy situations. Everyone spoke sign language on Martha's Vineyard. People did not think of or act toward people who could not hear as if they were deaf.

This has now changed because of the coming of tourists and other off-islanders, including an off-islander with a particular interest. Alexander Graham Bell came to Martha's Vineyard and discovered "deafness" there. Once discovered, there was no going back. Today, there are deaf people on Martha's Vineyard, as in the rest of the country. Groce's little book is eloquent testimony to disability as a social refraction of an interaction between the person and the environment.

Deborah A. Stone has written a succinct book, *The Disabled State,* that holds disability is a social category that did not always exist as we know it today. Once upon a time, Stone has it, there existed notions like lame, deaf, mute, halt, crippled, and others. Still, these did not coagulate into the modern category of disability until developments in the modern welfare state, itself a response to industrialization.

Every society has people who work and people who do not work. For example, in our society it is assumed that adults will work until retirement, while children will not work but go to school. Not working can be for an illegitimate reason, e.g. laziness, or for a legitimate reason, for example, being a single mother with a young child. The distinction between those who do not work for good reason and those who do not work out of laziness is crucial for the modern welfare state.

Stone points out that the welfare state has two large systems for distributing income, one wages, the other welfare. This is relevant to disability because disability is commonly assumed to be a valid reason for not working. How often have we heard politicians promise the voter that, if elected, every able-bodied person will work? It is a crucial question for the welfare state to grapple with: Who is able-bodied, and who is disabled?

If the modern welfare state was created as a response to industrialization, the modern category of disability was created for this response to industrialization. Before that, and before industrialization itself, disability, as we use that term today, did not exist. Today disability is central to many modern dilemmas of the welfare state.

There are other classics about disability. But these two suffice to suggest my point. I have also suggested that today the environment is largely the creation of persons and society. But these people and this society may not represent the wishes and interests of people with disabilities. People with disabilities may be marginal to an environment changed after the goals of other people.

Surely the evolution of the environment has been to make it more controllable by people. Roads make it possible to get from one place to another, telephone lines expand the range of the human voice, and the media improve on gossip. Change in the environment has not only been to make it more after the image of people, but has been to make it more under the control of people. Such change has always been important to people with disabilities. Eyeglasses and optics are one expression, wheelchairs another, the collapsible white cane often employed for guidance by individuals who are blind another.

The structure of the disabled person may place constraints on interaction with the environment that may make manipulating the environment as well as the person more important. Maybe a person with a disability is a square peg in a round hole. There may be just so far that one can go in shaving off the corners, in modifying the person to fit an environment, before the person loses spirit or becomes sullen. A person with a disability is often less flexible than an able-bodied sister or brother. Here is not only an intellectual justification for environmental change, but a practical one.

A square peg will not fit into a round hole, but it may squeeze into an octagonal hole. That is to say, if the environment is suitably modified, complementary adaptations in the person can make for good fit. Each instance should be judged on its own. Guidelines for matching people with disabilities with personal computers are only general guidelines.

Maybe you can't teach an old dog new tricks, but with human beings often you can. Attitudes can change profoundly. Recollect when we reckoned the worth of cars by size and chrome. Today the criteria have changed. This sort of malleability in attitude makes for the markets that drive technological change.

A consequence of disability expressing a relationship between a person and the environment is that it draws our attention to the interface between the person and the environment. A personal computer can be considered such an interface. We do not care here if a person can climb a flight of stairs, lift more than ten pounds, or has a low enough blood pressure. Disability, a relationship to the environment, through the interface of a computer is presented as a matter of input, output, or throughput.

For using a computer, we care about disabilities of input that involve entering information into the computer; disabilities of output that make it difficult for a person to obtain feedback from the computer, usually because of a learning disability or a visual disability;

and disabilities of throughput that may be less obvious and more recalcitrant. These throughput disabilities involve "processing information" and may occur with mental retardation or emotional disturbance. Learning disabilities may be thought of as throughput disabilities but more characteristically are expressed as input or output disabilities or a combination.

In sum, it is unnecessary to attach disabilities in input, output, and throughput to various conventional labels. In practice, of interest is interaction with the computer.

Understanding disability by input and output is written into the guidelines for Section 508 of the Rehabilitation Act of 1986 which would make computers purchased by the Federal Government usable or readily made usable by people with disabilities.

There is no discussion of throughput here. This is the most problematic of the three categories. And there is no straightforward correspondence between the needs of computer use and of throughput disability. Throughput disability may well be a little more than a metaphor, an object for research.

What follows are from the guidelines for Section 508 (a)(1) of Public Law 99-506. The section of the guidelines that follows is a specification of disability relevant to employee computer use.

1. Input

Access problems concerning the input interface to a microcomputer differ by the type and severity of the functional limitation of the employee. Some users with disabilities can use the keyboard if it can be modified slightly. Users with more severe disabilities require an alternate input strategy.

a. Modified Standard Keyboard Controls. The minimum access requirements for users of a modifiable, but standard keyboard, could be achieved by providing the following capabilities:

(1) Multiple Keystroke Control. Currently there are numerous common functions on the computer that require multiple, simultaneous keystrokes (e.g., to reboot a user could depress CTRL, then ALT, then DEL).

(2) Keyboard Repeat Rate. Currently the computer generates repetition of a character if the key is held down. This is a problem for those users without sufficient motor control of

their fingers to conform to the repeat tolerances of the keyboard. This feature would give the user control over the repeat rate. The user could extend the keyboard tolerance or turn off the repeat function completely.

(3) Input Redundancy. Currently numerous programs use a mouse as one of the input options. As the use of graphics increases so will dependence on the mouse as an input device. Some users with motor disabilities cannot use a mouse. This feature would provide an emulation of the mouse using the keyboard and/or other suitable alternative input devices, for instance, joy stick, trackball, voice input, and touch pad. In effect, any movement control executed through the mouse could also be executed from alternative devices.

(4) Toggle Keystroke Control. Currently toggle keys are employed which require visual feedback to know if a key is on or off. This feature would provide an alternative mode that does not require visual feedback to know the status of any toggle key.

b. Alternative Input Devices. The capability to connect an alternative input device would be available to the user who is not able to use a modified, but standard keyboard. This feature would supplement the keyboard and any other standard input system used. The alternative input capability would consist of a physical port (serial, parallel, game, etc.) or connection capability so that an accommodation aid could augment the keyboard or replace it. The computer would regard this device as its keyboard and the user would be able to input any valid keystroke combination (e.g., CTRL + ALT + DEL) available from the regular keyboard. This alternative input capability would also support the mouse emulation described above.

c. Keyboard Orientation Aids. There are several different keyboards available for current personal computers. To orient a visually impaired user to a particular keyboard, a set of tactile overlays should be available to identify the most important keys (e.g., ESC, ENTER, CTRL, ALT, and several key letters and numbers). The tactile overlays might be keycap replacements or transparent sticky tape with unique symbols to identify the various keys. To assist a motor disabled user, a keyguard should be available to ensure that the correct keys are located and depressed. A keyguard is a keyboard template with holes corresponding to the location of the keys which is placed over the keyboard.

2. *Output*

a. Auditory Output Capability. The auditory output capability on current personal computers is sufficient to keep and play music. Some users with disabilities, however, may require speech capability. For speech to be generated on today's computers, a speech synthesizer is required. The capability to support a speech synthesizer must continue to be available in future generations of computers or this capability must be internalized through an upgrade of the computer's internal speaker. Regardless of the methodology chosen, the volume should be adjustable by the user and a headset jack should be available.

b. Information Redundancy. Currently, several programs use the speaker to beep warnings or errors to the user. Some programs do not have the capability to present the warning visually to the hearing impaired user. This feature would allow the user to have information redundancy by presenting a visual equivalent of the beep on the monitor. This might be accomplished by either a manual screen indicator (one in which the user would have to indicate that he/she has seen the warning indicator by entering a key sequence to remove the indicator from the screen) or an automatic screen indicator (the warning would be presented for a period of time and then removed automatically).

c. Monitor Display. The requirement to enhance text size, verbally reproduce text, or modify display characteristics is crucial for some users with disabilities. To ensure that this access continues the following capabilities are required:

(1) Large Print Display. This feature increases the size of the portion of the screen for the low vision user. The process might use a window or similar mechanism that allows magnification to be controlled by the user. The user could invoke the large print display capability from the keyboard or control pad for use in conjunction with any work-related applications software. If applications software includes graphics, then enlargement of graphics should also be available.

(2) Access to Screen Memory for Text. The capability to access screen memory is necessary to support the speech and/or tactile braille output requirement of many blind users. Currently, blind users are able to select or review the spoken or braille equivalent of text from any portion of the screen while using standard application software. The nature of the access to the contents of the screen must continue to provide third party

vendors the capability to direct it to an internal speech chip, a speech synthesizer on a serial or parallel port, or a braille display device.

(3) Access to Screen Memory for Graphics. Information that is presented graphically also needs to be accessed from screen memory in such a manner that as software sophistication improves, it may eventually be interpreted into spoken output.

(4) Cursor Presentation. Where cursors or other indicators on the screen blink, the end user should be able to adjust the blink rate. This feature accommodates persons with seizure disorders who may be sensitive to certain frequencies of flashing light.

(5) Color Presentation. Here colors must be distinguished in order to understand information on display, colorblind end users should be able to select the colors displayed.

3. Documentation

The vendor will maintain a copy of all current user documentation on a computer, and will be responsive in supplying copies of this documentation in ASCII format suitable for computer-based auditory screen review or brailling.

Understanding disabilities by input, output, and throughput is novel and leads to novel results not the least of which is a recalibration of disability. As computers become more vital to the world, disabilities will become computer disabilities to an extent not now predictable.

Technology can truncate human potential instead of augmenting it. Used in modern bureaucracies, technology, in ways Max Weber foresaw, can turn people into, using the term coined in the twenties by Czech playwright Karel Capek, "robots."

Disability and technology may seem autonomous and self-contained. We are likely to regard disability as a property within a person, independent of environment and society. So too, are we likely to regard technology as existing apart from society, indeed as driving society and the environment.

If we reckon technology and disability as opposite, we can also reckon them as close. (Freud showed how close opposites can be.) Technology may be the cure to disability, as indeed it is to limitation, disease, and finitude.

Technology and disability are similar in that we seem certain about what they mean. This certainty dissolves upon inspection. Are we talking about high tech or low tech? What degree of bodily impairment constitutes a disability? We do not even know the answer to basic questions such as, Does technology drive society? or, Does society drive technology?

We talk about one technology, computing, and more particularly, the personal computer, the networks that make it accessible, the markets through which it is delivered, the education in which its use is taught, and the configuration, adaptation, and modification by which it is brought to bear on people with disabilities.

Increasingly, military strength has come through technology, relative military strength through relative technological superiority. The effects of technology on the soldiers who fight wars have been profound, especially in the area of disability. Modern technologies have made it possible to return fewer dead from the battlefield and more people with disabilities. We feel a special obligation to those who incur disability in military service. Many advances in social policy concerning disability have followed wars.

It may be harder for some persons with a disability to change as rapidly as others can. Perhaps spirit and body can only bend so far. The claims of a technological world are demanding for some people with disabilities. Let us examine some myths.

Myth 1: People with disabilities have easy access to the technology that they need.

Several years ago, in a presentation for a White House Conference, the purpose of which was to increase access to technology, the Trace Center estimated that of three million people who stood to gain from computing technology, only twenty thousand had personal computers.

That was guesswork, and surely the situation has improved today. The order of magnitude is probably unchanged. Only some people with disabilities standing to benefit from personal computers have them. Let us mention some reasons:

A. We know how difficult it is to bring computers into the office. Resistance to computers occurs, and they are often painful before they pay off. If, in the corporate setting, technological change is often difficult, why expect the experience of people with disabilities to be easier?

B. Access to computers for people with disabilities might lag, as people with disabilities have lagged in the receipt of other social resources, such as income, education, or integration.

C. The user sometimes does not buy the product; a third party buys it. This is a classic public policy problem with well known opportunities for market imperfections.

D. The socialization of people with disabilities may be such that they are less likely to know about innovations than their ablebodied peers, and this is true with computing technology. Not surprisingly, there has been no groundswell of demand.

E. People with disabilities tend to be poorer than people without disabilities. This reinforces their reliance on third party payers and disenfranchises them from a dollar vote in the market.

Myth 2: There is a market for technology amongst disabled people.

This is a myth for reasons stated above. Further, few people with disabilities are being matched with appropriate computing technology. Yet, what was true yesterday and today need not be true tomorrow.

Myth 3: There will never be a market worthy of attracting attention, except among manufacturers of specialty items for disabled people.

If this is true today, it need not be true tomorrow. To be this misled is to miss a significant marketing opportunity with disabled people. While a market for computers scarcely exists now, it may not take the genius of Henry Ford to create it.

One of the forces making a market possible is that personal computers are getting easier to use for everyone. More often than not, a computer that is easier to use will be easier to use for a disabled person as well. There are exceptions. Blind people, who benefitted immensely from computing technology in the recent past, have cause to feel threatened by graphic interfaces.

The general evolution is clear: the modern microcomputer, rapidly becoming cheaper and smaller, is itself a device that for many disabled people is a doorway to the world they can interact with. Yet personal computers and other technology do not unequivocally drive society, rather society drives computers as well. Marketing influences technological development.

Myth 4: The private sector will make advanced technology accessible to people with disabilities without any assistance or encouragement.

We do not expect this of the private sector with regard to our armed forces or space program. The cooperation of the public sector with the private sector has been evident since before the early days, with the Bureau of the Census. The public and private sectors are too intertwined to expect either to go it alone. The question is not whether they interact, but how they are to interact.

Myth 5: The public sector itself should make computers accessible to people with disabilities.

In this country the public sector is rarely invested with the ability to generate products, and that is the end of the myth. Largely the public sector has tasks like education, rehabilitation, defense, and other services. With respect to computers and disability, this role has not been fulfilled. Exactly how the public and private sectors ought to cooperate is a complex problem, which, however, cannot be left to chance.

Myth 6: The whole thing is best left to charity.

To do so is to relegate disabled people to a place outside of normal social mechanisms for dealing with human beings and elevate them to sainthood or debase them. Enlightened public and private policies will allow neither to happen.

Myth 7: A disability is a quality of a person, inside the person, and possessed by the person.

It is possible to take such a view and be consistent about it. Yet technology challenges it. These developments and common sense suggest that a disability is better viewed as a relationship between a person and environment.

Modern technology promises to change what we mean by disability. It could not do so were disability a property of a person (unless the technology were medical). Yet technology of all sorts is redefining the way we think about disability. Personal computers are capable, to a considerable extent now and in the future to a greater extent, of adapting to input, throughput, and output so that what may be a disability today may not be a disability tomorrow. Possible is a world where a disability is transformed from its industrial definition into a technological definition, in the process opened to further transformations.

Electronic architectures are cheaper to modify than physical architectures. Many electronic architectures needed and envisioned are yet to be built. Not only are we looking at a future where disability is defined differently from now, but a future where technologically enabling environments can increasingly eliminate much of disability.

Pioneering legislation, Section 504 of the Rehabilitation Act of 1973 and Public Law 94-142, The Education for All Handicapped Children's Act of 1975 speak of "reasonable accommodation," "least restrictive environment," "otherwise qualified handicapped individual." Computers and other electronic architectures have changed these terms. What may have been less reasonable before the age of technological enablement is so now. (For example, a blind person might not have been qualified with regard to certain employment. The arrival of large display and talking computers changes qualification.)

Often, appropriate environments have become interpreted by the courts in relationship to cost. Costly modifications of the environment often become cheaper with the new technologies of enablement. For example, many universities are installing scholar workstations to allow students access to information from diverse sources through electronic technology. It is reasonable that these scholar workstations be accessible to disabled people. The marginal cost is trivial, and access by disabled people usually does not diminish the work stations' usefulness to able-bodied people.

The first important step is to define disability in relationship not only to physical environments but to electronic ones. The second step is to make the environments adapt more and more to disabled people. This will change the shape of disability forever.

People

I was the first director of the Center for Computing and Disability, which I established in 1984. From its inception, my vision of the Center was that it serve not only students with disabilities on the Albany campus of the State University of New York where it is located and where I am on the faculty, but also other constituencies.

As I saw it the Center had to be a model project replicable elsewhere, and on campus this signified the project had to be one of quality carried forth with ethical commitment. I am pleased that the Center has been able to serve people with disabilities and the organizations that are there for them throughout the state, and that it has been a model for other centers. As I saw it the Center had to have an effect on public policy. Indeed it did.

The Center, among many other things, matches people with disabilities with appropriate computing equipment. The Center worked with the State Education Department, offered courses to vocational rehabilitation counselors, and developed a reputation for rigor, for suggesting only what was necessary in computing equipment. In addition to serving the tax payer, this has meant that the Center's matches have usually been funded by third parties.

Although I have explored some such matches in a chapter of that name, Matching, the range of disabilities and people is sufficiently large so as to make further discussion of other people appropriate.

They might be called cases. Yet to do so is to lose sight of the most important thing of all, which is that people come first. Technology enters only insofar as it serves people.

There is little room for medical labels (important as these are to medicine), traditional educational classifications (interesting though they may be to education), labels of functional impairment (significant though they may to vocational rehabilitation), and so on. I often disregard such information, although it routinely comes. The questions appropriate to matching a person with a disability to appropriate computing systems are of a different sort. I use first names (not real ones) in the stories that follow, for consistency and because that was frequently the atmosphere in which the work of the Center was carried out.

One day a man in a formidable looking electric wheelchair rolled into the Center. His name was Jim Dean.

It is instructive to dwell on the technology of the electric wheelchair. The technology necessary to build an electric wheelchair has existed for years. It was not put into effect until relatively recently. For many people, electric wheelchairs work splendidly. What happened?

It took a while to recognize that there was a market for electric wheelchairs and a while to convince third party payers to pay for them. It took a while to encourage demand and awareness of their possibilities by disabled people and their friends. Sound familiar? Just the sort of thing we are experiencing with regard to computer technology.

Initially there was a reluctance on the part of some to suggest them except for some people with little prospect for use of their arms Why? Because if someone has some use of his or her arms a good way to increase use is by exercise and a good exercise is operating a manual wheelchair. New technology makes things too easy. Sound familiar? The same often holds true with personal computers. Using a personal computer is a way to cheat on many tasks from arithmetic to organizing ideas coherently in one's head to remembering. But surely the point with the electric wheelchair is that it is a means to an end, mobility for the person with a disability, and the same with a computer, enablement for the person with a disability.

Jim Dean had sufficient control of his fingers to operate the joy stick on the electric wheelchair. Might some version of the joy stick be an appropriate input device for a computer? It seemed promising. I asked Jim to show me how the wheelchair moved. He had problems making it go the way he wanted. I judged the control insufficient to serve as an input to a computer.

Why do I have the right to make such a significant decision without even telling the person affected that I am making it? Why didn't I suggest a course of physical therapy that may have eventuated in the control required for using a computer? I would have preferred to educate Jim to know what I know, let him make the decision himself. I didn't have the option. Jim was here for a computer. To send him out the door without a computer would do no service. If a computer was appropriate for him, it was important that he get it.

I asked him what he could move. A couple of fingers and his head. I asked him to show me. The fingers didn't move much. "Can you move them any more?" I asked. He repeated the earlier motion. I asked him to move his head. "Move it from side to side as far as you can. Good. Now slowly. Good. Now stop when I say to. Good. Now move your head up and down."

The Apple Macintosh has a graphical user interface that is attractive and intuitive. Much of its operation is by pointing a device called a mouse and clicking on icons and words.

The graphical user interface makes the mouse a powerful input device. There are many devices that emulate mice, like track balls, joy sticks, touch pads. Several years ago, Personics marketed an outrageous device with an outrageous advertisement showing an outrageous maniac zooming along on his Macintosh. The device did not sell.

Apple directed Personics' attention to people with disabilities with good control of only their heads. This "flying mouse" changed its name from the *View Control System* to *HeadMaster* and its price multiplied by a factor of ten. With the *HeadMaster,* one points one's head at where one wishes the arrow (mouse cursor) to go. One can click with a puff and sip switch.

I set Jim up with one and in five minutes he was good and getting better. To enter text one can display a keyboard on the screen, point the arrow to the letter one wishes to type, and sip on the switch or hold the arrow there long enough for a timer to trigger the keystroke.

Jim was about to embark on a higher education, a prudent choice for many people with disabilities. Although the choice of a computer is often coupled with the choice of a career, this was premature in the case of Jim who did, however, express an interest in architecture. We matched him not only to a Macintosh and a *HeadMaster* but to a variety of other software and hardware that made it possible to study architecture as well as other subjects.

Here is a list of the items with which we matched Jim Dean:

1. *Pearl Corder* (voice activated tape recorder).
2. Macintosh SE with 20 megabyte hard disk.
3. *HeadMaster* (electronic head mouse).
4. *ImageWriter II* printer.
5. 2400 baud "Hayes Compatible" external modem with "System Peripheral-8″ cable.
6. Appropriate furniture for using the system. A computer desk was not necessary, only a table of appropriate height and size.

7. Miscellaneous computer supplies such as paper and ribbons.

There would be changes with a list made out today. Again, computer technology changes quickly. The SE is no longer made. The *Macintosh Classic* that has replaced it at half the price might better be passed over for a new middle range Macintosh with a color monitor. Still, although no one would buy this system today, it remains a fully useful system.

When to buy a rapidly changing technology is a difficult question for anyone. For a disabled person, the answer must be almost always now because of the grand benefit to be derived from computing. Naturally, there will be changes in the future. But this must be overlooked when benefits are to be derived in the present.

Wherever possible and prudent I draw the attention of the purchasing agency to the least expensive place to buy appropriate technology. New York State has a state contract system that is available to many agencies. I also concluded that a voice operated tape recorder was appropriate to Jim, that is item 1 above. Item 5 is a modem. This hardware, with appropriate software, allows a computer to talk with any other computer likewise equipped over an ordinary telephone line. Disabled people may want to do this for the same reasons as anyone: transferring files, saving messages, collaborating on work, working at home, accessing bulletin boards, etc. People with mobility impairments may find it particularly useful to do many things from home that would otherwise require moving around. To an extent, transportation can be replaced by communications.

In order to accomplish the immediate tasks and some probable tasks facing Jim Dean in the near future, we recommended the following software (a list that would change somewhat today):

1. *MicroSoft Works*
2. McIntyre *WordWriter* software
3. *SuperPaint*
4. *Super3D*
5. *SideKick for the Macintosh*
6. *Doug Clapp's Word Tools*
7. *Spelling Coach Professional*
8. *Symantec Utilities for Macintosh (SUM II)*

This software list is not complete. Should Jim end up in, say, accounting, he will need other software. Yet the software is adequate for present and foreseeable needs. It does not make sense to purchase specialized software which are likely to be improved on before Jim uses them. A system to cover every eventuality is impossible. Not everything can be done at once. For some things, Jim has to wait.

The software included utilities, a spelling checker, address list, telephone dialer, a word processor, and other features. Item number 2 on the list immediately above merits explanation. *WordWriter* is out of the University of Utah and puts a keyboard on the screen. One types a letter with the *HeadMaster* (by positioning the mouse cursor on a letter and clicking), and a list of words beginning with the letter typed appears on the screen. One need only select the word. Even this elementary lexical prediction cuts down on input.

I have the pleasure of teaching a class on computing and disability. This class is partly about what personal computers can do for people with disabilities. I talk about various modifications that can be made to a computer. I talk about what a personal computer can do for people in general and for people with disabilities in particular. Some of the class is hands-on experience with a computer.

Much of it is about other aspects of disability touched on in this book without which computers become mere technology. The class is first about people; technology enters only insofar as it can help people.

Various moves encourage a spirit of "can do," pride, and cooperation. One such move is the integration of the class to include people with disabilities and present and future disability professionals. They learn from each other and teach each other in an experience valuable for both.

I have discovered a new disability, computerphobia. Increasingly, it can be debilitating. The class has some computerphobes each semester.

People with disabilities who take the class are often unaware of what computers can do for them and often unaware that computers can be modified to be more accessible. These students are educated in both and leave the class knowing what sort of personal computer to be thinking about. Since they have worked on it, the results are more satisfactory than a simple match. Since the education that must follow a match has been started, matches are more successfully connected to the rest of life.

For example, one person who took the class was Gene. I would come to know some things about Gene during the course of the term. He spoke a lot. He was enthusiastic. He knew little about computers and only about his own disability, not about disability in general. He had a wife and three children. He had a full-time job. It was a joy to see his self confidence grow along with his mind.

He had a visual impairment about which two things are important. It was stable, and it required that the monitor image be substantially enlarged. Dr. Carolyn Forsberg and Carol Connoly were teaching the class with me. I cannot remember if it was Dr. Forsberg or I who thought that Gene should learn how to use a screen reader on a device that speaks the text on the screen, using a synthesized voice together with the image enlarger. I am certain that it was Dr. Forsberg who concluded that it was appropriate that Gene learn how to use the screen reader first.

Many people with visual disabilities do not benefit from enlarging the characters on the screen, however large, the images remaining difficult or impossible to decode. Other people with visual disabilities do benefit from enlarging the screen.

Still other people benefit from both a screen reader and an image enlarger. Gene was one of these. There were times when the screen reader was more efficient, and times when the image enlarger was more efficient. For Gene they complemented each other. It was Dr. Forsberg's inspiration to teach him the screen reader first. There was a purpose to this. In general, the screen reader takes longer to learn to use. With an image enlarger an easy way out, a person might not be willing to invest the time. It was her decision that Gene would lose from this.

Anybody who has not grown up with them and tries to use them knows that at the beginning computers are brilliant at complicating your life. At the beginning, computers make things harder, not easier. This is true even for straightforward applications like word processing. It is enough to make many forego computing.

What is true for able-bodied people may be even truer for disabled people. Many people with disabilities not only must learn how to use computers but how to use adaptive devices. Many adaptive devices are difficult to learn to use. Frustration is sane.

During the first class I explain that, for a while, personal computers may make things harder. I promise light at the end of the tunnel. If I were a student, I don't think I would believe me.

But frustration is difficult for a teacher to bear in a student; patience is an obligation. Sooner or later, computers pay off and adaptive solutions pay off. Gene had to work a while to learn how to use the screen reader. He proved to be a gutsy person and plowed through and mastered it.

Had I simply seen Gene outside of the class contacts and matched him with a screen reader and an image enlarger, I could never have been sure that the match was optimal. Dr. Forsberg's strategy of screen reader first would have been hard to implement. Knowing Gene as I do now, things would have worked out. For many people with disabilities, however, there is less cause for comfort in a match, however deft. The match is best followed by an education that occurs within the context of a life.

In class there is time to try out more solutions for a longer time, less need to rely on my intuition and knowledge. An active partner in the match, the student can be educated to become his or her own advocate. If a professional, he or she has a chance to learn about personal computers in context applied to different people.

The University at Albany is computer accessible to students with disabilities. Although college campuses are almost always aware of issues of architectural accessibility, computer accessibility may be less salient even as computers are becoming more integral to a university education. It is not only students who need educating, but universities as well.

A University at Albany student who is disabled has appropriate computing technology accessible to her or him at the university. Computers may be more important to a disabled student than to an able-bodied student. Relying on university computers may thus be as peculiar as relying on the university for pencils and on the library for texts. The same holds true with K–12 education and even earlier. Having one's own personal computer is bizarre (perhaps) only because it seems expensive. Yet for a person with a disability the benefits of a personal computer may well outweigh the cost, which pales anyway next to the cost of education.

Who is to pay? Students and their families are frequently in debt. Students with disabilities may find it difficult to get part-time work. All the more reason that computing systems be specified that are as inexpensive as possible and yet can do what needs to be done. A third party may pay. Sometimes medical insurance, sometimes vocational rehabilitation, sometimes relatives. Always as inexpensive as possible, as powerful as necessary.

Fortunately, the cost of personal computers has sunk (and is sinking) sufficiently to often make this workable. I suggest that the number of third parties be increased, that universities at least provide access to personal computers to disabled students as part of a reasonable accommodation, that the K–12 system supply them as a necessary part of education, and that employers provide them for employees with disabilities.

Gene had a job. Like most people with disabilities with a job, he will have to pay for a personal computer himself. For Gene and his family this will be a hardship. Gene's children will not wear the clothes that Gene and his wife would like nor play with the toys in vogue amongst their friends. Yet Gene is convinced that a personal computer is a necessary if not sufficient condition to get some of what he would like his family to have. This is a hard choice for Gene.

One of the first people with whom I matched a computer was Ed, a seven-year-old with fixed ideas. Sometimes fixed ideas, and even a certain obnoxiousness, serve children with disabilities well, as they are apt to get bounced around a bit. Ed had one of the many sorts of cerebral palsy. A catch-all diagnosis at best, it was of no particular interest to me. Observation revealed that he had difficulty using his hands to type.

Ed came with his mother and his occupational therapist. He was sent on the recommendation of his principal who looked at computers as a way to mainstream Ed. Mainstream means integrate and derives *inter alia* from Public Law 94-142, The Education for All Handicapped Children Act. This act was a civil rights act by design. Arguably, its present-day interpretation is a devaluation of its original intent.

All too frequently the formidable array of people that supported Ed is lacking. What can be done then can only be done by mobilizing appropriate people in the life of the student with the disability. Computers are good for mobilizing people. No need for that here; Ed was lucky.

Although he had difficulty typing, his occupational therapist insisted that he make whatever use of his hands he had. I found a deep desire to communicate in Ed. His speech was impaired, which made the desire to communicate all the more profound. I gave Ed an unsharpened pencil, which he held in his teeth. It turned out he could be very accurate with it.

Pencils are inexpensive. They are remarkable devices, even when turned backwards. A shaft of wood, usually just the right length, is firmly connected to a rubber device that is unlikely to slip. His occupational therapist was horrified at the pencil.

I reasoned that Ed was only seven. He had many years to learn to type, but typing was a means to an end, and that was communication. If cut off from communication now, there was no predicting the deleterious effects. Communication came first. Anything that encouraged it was fair game. He would have time enough to learn to use his hands more.

The occupational therapist and I were at odds. Clearly, as soon as they left the room, the occupational therapist would have the authority. It would be fruitless for me to impose my will while they were in the room. Deliberately, I spoke to the mother, telling her why I thought the pencil appropriate. She smiled and said that she had been thinking that communication was the first priority for some time. In fact, she knew some other mothers with children with disabilities who felt the same way, and who regarded some well-meaning attempts to "normalize" their children as counterproductive, ultimately leading to less normalization.

I had connected with a deep intuition on the part of the mother. Matching sessions must be used for more than matching. Attempts to impose solutions will fail one way or the other.

So Ed would use a pencil. He smiled as I asked him if he wanted a color monitor. A next door neighbor to me was home-bound. He was on welfare but had a 25-inch color television, an obvious waste of welfare money. Every Saturday and Sunday people used to come from near and far to watch the week's game on his glorious TV, which, on second thought, may not have been a waste of money. He was happy and ingenious.

My neighbor in mind, I suggested a color monitor for Ed. I also suggested some games, a word processor, and an input device that would not disable the keyboard. I wanted other kids to gather around his computer. I insisted that he have his own personal computer, not merely access to a class computer or a school computer.

I connected a Keytronics keyboard with a touch keypad and put a few " x 's" on its keypad. I asked him to bop them. Success! I promised him that when he came back, the keypad would have the letters of the alphabet on it and, further, these letters (and symbols) would be marked so the most frequently hit would be at the center of the keypad, the most infrequently hit would be at the edges. His mother thought that was a good idea. He would use the keypad, and his teachers and the other kids would use the keyboard.

That evening I called my niece. I asked her if she would take out her scrabble game, write down the value of each letter, and mail them to me on a postcard. Two days later the postcard arrived and programming the keypad became a class project. What came out of this was elegant.

But I had outsmarted myself. Ed has never used the keypad, partly because he already knew where the keys were on the keyboard, and partly because he did not want to be more different from his friends than necessary. I make fewer such mistakes today. Cuteness is to be avoided, even if slightly better.

Ed necessarily did not look at the screen while typing. Thus he had an output disability. The reason that he did not look at the screen was that he was looking at the keys. It is difficult to look at the screen if you are typing with a pencil between your teeth.

This is true of many people with input disabilities. One solution is *Turbo Lightning*. This will beep if you misspell a word. Another is to hook up a screen reader to read back the letters as you type them. The first solution is cheaper. It turned out to be satisfactory to Ed.

One afternoon Jerri came in for a match. She had lived in my neighborhood, and I knew her and her family. They had moved to the suburbs, and she had got hit by a car, resulting in brain injuries that affected her coordination and her thinking. Her coordination was a straightforward problem.

Being friends is regarded by some professionals as somehow injurious. Usually, it isn't. In the case of matches, it surely isn't.

My resourceful assistant, Bruce Bailey, and I matched Jerri with an adaptive software package called *Filch*. *Filch* is a simple and elegant package that does many things, including allowing for serial input of CONTROL, ALT, and SHIFT keystroke combinations, audible beeps after letters, an increase in the time a key must be pressed to activate the computer — which frequently takes care of the problem of touching other keys on the way to the key one wants. Many things considered, *Filch* is a useful package designed particularly for people with disabilities.

What to do with Jerri's throughput disabilities? She was seven years old, an age that would allow her to grow up with computers and probably get to know how to use them better than a grown person. Yet her mind would change; computers would change; theories of how to educate children with throughput disabilities would change. What in the future? We did nothing special now except, importantly, match her with a computer.

We matched her with some appropriate software, including games. Of course the screen was colored, and, since I am cowardly about children's eyes, it was high resolution VGA. No one should have to handle floppy disks, particularly a child with a disability. I matched Jerri with a hard disk large enough not only for her current software but for future software.

It had been an earlier experience that often the people responsible for the purchase of a personal computer end up buying something different from what we recommend. At times they are able to do better and cheaper, but with all humility, that is extremely rare. Frequently, the systems they end up with will not do the job. Sometimes, they are more expensive than necessary. Always, they take longer to purchase. On occasion they sit on a shelf waiting for someone to put the parts together.

I like to think of computers as can openers. They are useful not only for what they can do themselves for the person with the disability, but in changing the whole system. In schools, they can help not only to enable students but to empower parents and teachers.

Matching a person with a disability with a personal computer is the easy part. But it is an important beginning. If done correctly, it can help lead to changes that benefit all. If done incorrectly, the can remains closed.

Word Processing

Word processing is nice. For many people with disabilities it is more than that. It is necessary. Even many people without disabilities regard it as essential. Widespread use of word processing by people with disabilities is overdue.

Whether we are an information society is an open question. Whether we are a society that depends on the written word is, however, a question whose answer is a given: we are, and to be unable to write in this society constitutes a form of disability, particularly painful in that it is so often unnecessary.

This disability is predicated on a social organization that has failed to meet the demands of literacy. Schools — inner city, suburban, small town, rural — fail at times. Special education programs may be a special failure, for here it is recognized (at least in theory) that something special is required, and yet, frequently, students emerge from special education without the skills of reading and writing.

The extent to which personal computers as word processors can rectify illiteracy is not altogether clear. The studies are just beginning. It makes intuitive sense that word processing has profound effects on the writing of everyone and on people with disabilities in particular. Research in progress as well as widely circulated anecdotes suggest the profound impact word processing can have on the writing of people with disabilities.

Often, word processing is the reason for acquisition of a personal computer, and sometimes word processing is the sole use of the computer. Word processing is a useful skill today, frequently offering the person with a disability an edge.

Computing has a significant role to play in the lives of people with disabilities, as in the lives of all. An appropriate entrance into the world of computer technology can be made through word processing. This chapter discusses word processing, what it is, what it has to offer, and some wrinkles and roses, for people with disabilities.

39

Although what follows concerns word processing, it is to be read in the context of computing in general. Word processing is not only an end in itself, but can raise questions about computing and point toward answers. From the point of view of the computer, word processing is simply an application.

Word processing, as will be seen here, and is seen better in actual practice, is a leap in writing from the typewriter which was a leap over the pen which was a leap from the hammer and chisel. Throughout recorded history, conveying thoughts to a reader has become easier and easier.

A person uses a word processor. What happens? I will call the person "Sue."

Sue uses the word processor most commonly through a keyboard that closely resembles that of a typewriter. There are some variations in positioning, e.g., of the BACKSPACE/DELETE key, CONTROL key, ALTernate key, and function keys. Still, it looks like an electric typewriter with TV, although the keyboard might well be detachable and, if Sue wants, she might perch it on her lap or in another position convenient to her.

There is no reason that the input device into the word processor should look like a typewriter keyboard — except convention. It is a workable convention for most people. Some people, stenographers for example, might prefer a radically different keyboard, one that looks like a stenotype. This would use a program that automatically expands stenographic notes into typewritten format.

In principle, although not always fact (yet), input could come by way of speech, electromyograph potential, eye movement, a pedal, or any of a variety of other devices. The only necessity is that the device be able to digitize the input — that is, be able to convert pressure from the fingers, the sound of a voice, or whatever, into a series of "yes"'s and "no"'s, or "on"'s and "off"'s, or "zero"'s and "one"'s. (If the input were in Morse code, it would already be digitized.) The input device is, to a certain extent, arbitrary, conventional, and fixed by habit. Yet it does not pay to break habit without a pressing reason.

Other features differentiate a word processor from a typewriter. The written material appears on a monitor which is a visual representation of what has been entered into the machine. For someone with visual or learning disabilities that make it difficult to acquire information, other forms of output may be required, e.g., image enlargement, voice output, braille output.

Having the text on a screen is less permanent than having it as ink on paper (or "hard copy"). It is easy to erase mistyped keystrokes, misspelled words, or words about which one has second thoughts. Two keys can do this. One is the BACKSPACE/DELETE key; the other is the DELETE key.

The function of the BACKSPACE/DELETE key is like in the game, PacMan: go back and gobble up letters. Thus, if you have hit an "L" when you mean to hit a "K," you may be conscious of this mistake as you make it. Pushing the BACKSPACE/DELETE key erases the "L" and moves you back into position to type the "K." For many people this makes typing quicker, since they do not have to be as concerned about errors.

Observing word processing by school children leads to the hunch that as the idea of "mistakes" is less hazardous, the child may be ready to take more risks. He or she may have a painful experience with errors, perhaps, marked with red " × "'s by teachers. At times, perhaps, he or she was afraid to write a sentence before thinking about it repeatedly. Redoing the sentence may have meant discarding the sheet of paper.

With disabilities, the odds of making a mistake are greater. To many people with disabilities, correcting mistakes is yet more disastrous. The virtue of easily rectifiable mistakes applies to all — but more so to people with disabilities.

Taught on word processors, a new generation of writers may well not have the idea of "mistake." Almost anything is modifiable and correctable with minimal effort.

Imagine the difference between a written page and a ticker tape. Both convey written language, but the ticker-tape must be read in a line, and to read it involves respooling the tape to find a point. With a page, one can scan up and down, left and right, right and left, down and up. The ticker-tape is linear, the page is two dimensional.

This two dimensional quality may be in the reading, but it does not figure in the writing. To write with a typewriter is to generate line after line of text, like a ticker-tape.

With a word processor, however, the two dimensional field is open. This has consequences. For instance, should a mistake occur anywhere in the text, it is a simple matter to go back and fix it with the word processor. And not only is a word processor nonlinear on the page, it allows one to jump from page to page.

Consider a few more examples. Rewriting is important to writing.

Using a word processor, rewriting, making changes, becomes easy. You move the cursor (the designator of action) to where you want to make the change, and delete, add, or revise.

The above examples, useful for anybody with a word processor, particularly somebody who is disabled, show mastery of the many techniques for moving the cursor around the page and through the document. Almost always, the following are possible:

> move the cursor space by space
> move the cursor word by word
> move the cursor line by line
> move the cursor to the end or beginning of the line
> move the cursor to the end or beginning of the paragraph
> move the cursor to the end or beginning of the page
> move the cursor to the end or beginning of the document

Many cursor moves require the use of more than one key concurrently, which may be difficult or impossible for some people with disabilities. If so, combine the word processing program with any of a number of programs that allow the SHIFT, ALT, and CONTROL keys to be pressed in sequence rather than simultaneously with other keys. This "one finger" mode makes available not only many moves of the cursor, but many other features of word processing as well. This is an example of the flexibility of word processing that allows one to electronically attach another piece of software—to add some special feature which may be required for the disabled person—to use with the word-processing software. Further ways to control the cursor include a mouse, difficult for some people with a disability, a trackball, and a touch pad. There are yet other devices.

A cursor movement particularly appropriate to some people with disabilities uses a search function to locate a string, or set of symbols, and automatically positions the cursor just there. This is often useful for the person with an output impairment, as a string can be located automatically without reading the text. For people with many disabilities such positioning of the cursor is accurate.

It is easy to change the order of words, sentences, paragraphs, and so on. It even is possible to transfer the order, read what you have written, decide that it is not best, revise it and revise it again until you have what you want. Of course, none of these revisions is entirely painless always.

However, for most people with disabilities, changes are often easier than entering text. Perfection is not as difficult as in the past.

With modern printers, especially modern laser printers, and various formatting features it becomes possible to turn out a document that looks so professional that it conveys the message, "Job Well Done."

Often, writing is less a steady stream and more gushes and dry spots. Word processors take advantage of the gushes. Take a chance. Leave a blank spot. Continue with another gush. How about another gush? Or would you prefer to digress to a different topic? Digressions are no problem. Although they may be irrelevant here, they can be shoved to the end of the document or pushed off into another document.

There are text data base management systems to help you keep track of such digressions, call them "ideas." For example, I have the option of discussing such text database management systems here or in another chapter. I do not have to make the choice now.

Text database management systems are free form and you can run searches without prespecified key words. Some database management systems are packaged integrally to word processing systems, such as *Nota Bene,* others are stronger on the text database management system and weaker on the word processing, such as *DayFlo.* Other systems, such as *ZY Index,* can be attached to existing word-processors, while others, like *Gofer,* allow searching through existing files. Many word-processors can search across files for words. There are many more TDBM systems on the market and still more under development.

It is possible not only to search words out, but to search for a combination of words. For instance, there are systems that will allow you to search for every instance in which you used the word "computer" within ten words of "disability."

These possibilities suggest the importation of existing data files into the word processing document on which you are working. Suppose you are doing a review of newspaper articles on China and technology in the *New York Times* in the last two years. A database contains the *New York Times,* and you could ask that it be searched for those references where China occurred within fifteen words of technology (or list some particular technologies if you wish). Suitable records could be loaded onto the disk on your personal computer and incorporated into your document as appropriate.

Some hold spelling to be a valuable skill. It may be, but it is less valuable than writing. As long as you are able to take an intelligent guess at what a word might be, you can use the spell checking function after the document to run through your document, picking out spelling errors and typographical errors. Not only is this valuable for the nondisabled typist, it may be invaluable to the typist with a disability.

There are spelling checkers that will beep when you make a spelling mistake or typo. Some people will find the beep a bother, other people will find the beep a blessing. Many blind or visually impaired people welcome the beep, as do many people with learning disabilities. (A software version of a beeping on-line spelling checker is Borland's *Turbo Lightning*.)

Useful to able-bodied people, even more valuable to many disabled people, is the computer thesaurus. The computer thesaurus is valuable to people who have difficulty with a paper thesaurus.

Not explicitly mentioned has been the initial entering of text into the computer; more has been said on ways of modifying text. But problems remain with the input. Some people just type slowly. There is a software package called *PRD +* that allows one to write a word in a recognized system of shorthand and the computer expands it automatically. Of course, there is a substantial learning curve here, and not everybody might find it worthwhile to learn shorthand to be able to write, just as not everybody may find it reasonable to touch type. Still some people with disabilities may find it invaluable.

A promising technique that extracts the most output from the least number of keystrokes is lexical prediction, as in the program *MindReader,* which can cut down keystrokes by 75 percent. Another lexical prediction program is produced by MacIntyre for use with Apple's Macintosh computers.

The ideal lexical predictor would read the mind of the writer. Currently the mind is "read" by picking up certain cues. What may happen is this: one types the letter "a" and is given a list of words beginning with the letter "a" that one could have meant; one types the second letter, "b," and is given a list of words that begin with "ab"; one types the letters "abo" and is given again a choice of words. One regards them as a menu and chooses, either by directing a cursor, by typing a number, or another form of menu selection.

Current lexical prediction is primitive. Unused thus far are any of the slew of grammatical rules now available to us as well as laws of probability, such as those used by IBM *VoiceType* and *Dragon Dictate*. We look forward to seeing this sophistication applied to the mundane task of generating menus that, for all their earthliness, could be a boon to some people with disabilities. Lexical prediction is a logical technique for getting maximum output from minimum input.

Lexical prediction is typical of many new solutions that are software-based rather than hardware-based. With new rapid microcomputers with large inexpensive memory it is possible to do with software what may previously have required hardware.

The move from dedicated word processors to word processing programs that can be run on any microcomputer is an example of a move from hardware to software. Instead of buying a machine that can word process and only word process, one buys software that allows a personal computer to word process. Software word processors usually allow for the insertion of one or another "one finger" programs, keyboard redefinition programs, programs that minimize some aspects of tremor, programs that read back the screen, and a catalog of other software of interest.

Outline processors provide an outline around which one can generate a document. These aids to thinking, writing, and organization may be of particular use to people with disabilities, especially those disabilities that make organization problematic, as with some forms of learning disabilities.

Additions to the basic word processor are many, including desktop publishers, controllers of laser printers, producers of various sorts of fonts and style sheets of particular use to those with disabilities where various formats — from a letter to a term paper to a memorandum — are invoked at the touch of several keystrokes. The selection of an appropriate word processor and word processing accessories is more complex than it might appear at first blush.

It is curious that modern word processing is the most visibly seductive use of the computer for many people with a disability, since word processing may often require many keystrokes for the amount of output (as compared to programming, spreadsheets, environmental control, etc.). Not puzzling is the observation with which this chapter opened. Writing is among the most important of skills for everybody. To be able to write fluently, efficiently, and clearly is an important skill demanded of most people in jobs involving thought.

To be unable to write is a disability for everyone. For a disabled person, not to be able to write is doubly disabling. The word processor can be of unique service.

Serendipity

Tomorrow, it will be a commonplace that computing has much to offer to people with disabilities. Today, it is a commonplace for some yet is unknown to others, who may discover it in the future. Yet this commonplace is remarkable for, after all, personal computers were not developed with people with disabilities in mind.

Even today, aside from a peripheral market of assistive devices, serendipity has marked the encounter of the technology, personal computers, and a group of people, those with disabilities, each having a separate and unique history.

It is an interesting and perplexing question as to why computers have so much to offer people with disabilities, or, why this particular technology among so many other technologies should have such a profound benefit.

Disability resides neither in a person nor in the environment, it is tensed between biology and society. Computing also is not autonomous. It did not spring full-grown from the head of science. Rather, computing, as other technologies, is tensed between science and society.

Numbers measure the world. The extension of numbers to increasing parts of the world is part of the history of science. Why there should be a connection between numbers and the world is a more profound riddle than why there should be a connection between computing and disability. It has led some scientists to believe in the existence of God. Virtually all mathematicians are Platonists, which is to say that they hold numbers and relationships between numbers to exist independently of what they measure.

In large measure, science is number applied to the world. Numbers are subject to all sorts of manipulations, and part of the history of mathematics, science, and technology has been to make such manipulations easier. Computers make computation easier.

There were predecessors in this endeavor. Imagine performing a

46

calculation with Roman numerals. How do you divide CXXIV by LVI? This was so complex that it absorbed much of the education of many a Roman. Matters were simplified with the importation of the Arabic numberals that gave different meanings to digits according to the place that they occupied. With such numerals and a means of writing (eventually pencil and paper), it became possible to perform calculations quickly and easily that would have taxed the mind and energy of someone using another notation.

For those not disposed to consider pencil, paper, and notation as the first computer, consider the abacus, which originated in Oriental society for mercantile use over 5000 years ago. In the Middle Ages it was used throughout Europe and Asia. It is still used.

In 1642 Blaise Pascal developed a device to assist in calculations for his father's business. It is perhaps curious that a philosopher should have developed such a device not for scientific use but for the use of the business.

A mathematician, competitor with Newton for the invention of the calculus, saw Pascal's machine and improved on it. Leibniz's step reckoner multiplied, divided, and could even reckon square roots. The first commercially available calculators were produced by Thomas Colmar in 1820.

Charles Babbitt conceived his "analytical engine" in the 1830s. This device not only computed, but had a memory, and made decisions based on its computations. Unfortunately, the device exceeded the capabilities of other technologies that had not achieved the precision necessary to build it.

Contributions to computing came by way of pure mathematics. In the mid–19th century, George Boole developed an algebra with just two digits, zero and one. This algebra had an uncanny affinity with the laws of logic, which led Boole to entitle his treatise on it, *The Laws of Thought*. It is important for the development of modern digital computers because they too use but two digits, zero and one — "switches," transmissive or not.

In 1880 the American statistician, Herman Hollerith developed the punched card. Where there was a hole, an electronic circuit was completed; where there was paper, it was interrupted. Its purpose was to work with the national census. The development of this technology was integrally related with the census and, by extension, with what census data are used for in society.

In the early 1800s, Joseph-Marie Jacquard had used punch cards to control the operation of a loom. Textiles were vital to a social innovation, the industrial revolution. Jacquard's invention can be thought of as the first robot, for the Jacquard loom used information to control physical process. The involvement of the Jacquard loom with society is obvious.

Shortly before World War II, an horrendous political and social conflict, the brilliant British mathematician, Turing, developed a machine on paper that was capable of using results in other calculations, a property known as recursiveness. Turing was to play an instrumental part in cracking the German code; in breaking this code, he shortened the war.

During World War II, American industry changed. Its connections with government increased. Another brilliant mathematician, von Neuman, contributed to the physical realization of the Turing Machine and further suggested the intriguing possibility that future computers could make computers. Already computers make and design much of what we consume, including much of computers. Von Neuman's science fiction is rapidly becoming reality.

In 1944, Howard Aiken of Harvard and a large corporation that had taken off with Hollerith in tabulating the census, International Business Machines, completed the construction of the Harvard Mark 1. This cooperation between academia and corporations, a social phenomenon, was to increase.

The early electronic computers used relays or vacuum tubes. The Mark 1 was followed by the ENIAC, which was followed by the EDVAC which was followed by the ORDVAC, Baldwin 1, and IBM 701. The UNIVAC I was constructed for the United States Bureau of the Census. The elements were in place for the computer as we know it today: calculating capability, memory, and operations controlled by a program.

Although electronics were far quicker than the earlier mechanical devices and had the capacity to do more, vacuum tubes still had a considerable response time, generated enormous quantities of heat that had to be dissipated, and took up much room. The next generation of computers took off in 1959, using the transitor as an alternative to the vacuum tube.

During the late 60s and 70s, the electronics were made smaller and quicker by the construction of the integrated circuit and then by the computer chip which allows for the replication of elaborate circuits in a small space.

The computer developed as a joint product of society and science. Society demanded enhanced computation, automation, counting, and control.

At first, the history of computers may seem to lack any connection to the history of disability except for the significant fact that both, to a large degree, are social. But the history of computing — and any technology — is a record of "disability" understood in the broadest perverse sense.

Thus, for example, the technology of cooking is predicated on people who are unable to chew what is tough, digest it, and savor it. The reason that we do not think of these people as "disabled," is that the "disability," so to speak, is shared by all human beings, and society does not reckon the disability.

Similarly, technologies of aeronautics help the "flying disabled" to take to the air. We could go on with building, armaments, etc. The technology of computing seeks to rectify the "disability" that so many of us have with complex calculations, and large memory.

The history of technology is an attempt to ease "disabilities" shared by the human race. Of course, to say this is to reveal immediately the social characteristics of disability. For the fact is, we consider a person disabled only if the disability occupies a special place in our social construction. This is what makes such a broad definition of disability perverse. We are not all "disabled." Disability, as commonly used, is an intellectual construction that we use to deal with certain classes of people.

But technologies developed to rectify a perverse notion of "disability" have had profound effects, mostly good, on those human beings commonly referred to as disabled. This spillover is a result of the effects that rectifying "disability" has on actual disability as we commonly understand the term. Technology has, more often than not, been of use to people whom we think of as disabled.

We possess much technology to accommodate people who are disabled. Whether it is used is still a question. If technology is ill distributed, many will still be excluded.

An understanding of the other side of technology is needed by everyone. There is much potential for abuse. In her book *The Electronic Sweatshop,* Barbara Garson speaks of the technology of computing used for control. She cites the examples of McDonald's, airline reservations, social work, the stock market, consulting, and the way we fight wars as having already provided evidence of computers as control devices.

Garson cites the pioneering work of David Noble, who chronicled the transition from the artisan tool and die maker to computer assisted design and manufacture. This transition, claims Noble, transformed the blue collar workplace, destroying a sanctuary of autonomy.

Whether such uses of computing technology, and technology in general, will be used to control people is, according to Garson and Noble, an open question. Others, such as the French writer Jacques Ellul, have claimed it to be inevitable. In his book *The Technological Society,* Ellul claims to demonstrate the implacable domination of technology over society. If the views of Garson and Noble are correct, we have a choice in the use of technology.

The implications of this choice for dealing with disability are vast. We can use our choice by adapting the technology that shapes the environment in which it is imbedded. In the future a society that allocates its technology democratically and fairly can be one in which disability, as we commonly know it, will cease to exist.

If technology is coming to control the physical world, the problem ever more is to control the world inhabited by people, and thus the technology. This involves not brute force or power, but rather subtler knowledge, education, and information. This development plays to a particular strength in the human species, its intellect.

Computers are presently narrow aids to the intellect. As aids to intellect, computers have much to offer and the importance of manipulable electronic architectures in an information society is especially marked for people with disabilities.

The world becomes overwhelmingly an information environment. A person using a computer is frequently expected to provide a final product, itself information, to be displayed before consumers or other people in what may be a complex organization where the person with a disability works. But frequently information can be electronically modeled, and modified, by the computer. Such manipulation allows for flexibility for anyone.

Take word-processing, described in an earlier chapter. What is entered into the computer does not become hard copy. Rather, it becomes an electronic model amenable to change from the BACKSPACE/DELETE, to moving paragraphs around, to formatting. All can be done simply. What is true for word processing is true with accounting, computer-assisted design, programming, and countless other applications.

Personal computers can be linked together in local area networks or by modem to any other computer with modem in the world. Communications and networking are yet other enabling features of computing for disabled people.

A future where robots (computers attached to devices capable of acting in the physical world) exist is partly present. Robots can help people with disabilities.

The vision of computer giving birth to computer signals the possibility of a new species (predicated on silicon and gallium much as humans and animals are predicated on organic carbon). Such a species could make things difficult for the human race and social precautions extending beyond Isaac Asimov's three laws of robotics are necessary for a human relation with robots.

Enough science fiction. The computer world as it is offers many new opportunities to people with disabilities. What is continuously required are the social organization, education, politics, public policy, entrepreneurship, and other mechanisms necessary to provide these opportunities—especially to people who heretofore have been underrepresented in social and political processes.

Although the price of computers will decrease dramatically, the price of getting the appropriate hardware and software to people with disabilities, teaching them how to use it, teaching teachers, in short, the social infrastructure accompanying the use of computers, will increase enormously.

Currently, we spend little on the delivery of computing to people with disabilities. One consequence is that few people with disabilities are aware of what computing can do for them; even fewer are in a position to acquire and learn to use this equipment. But the issue is not only the social cost involved in delivering new service, but the ultimate savings to be realized by such delivery. Common sense tells us that savings will be large and potentially enormous.

A question to be asked about a future where people with disabilities have significant and advantageous access to appropriate computing technologies is not whether technology in the future will have changed—it will. It is whether the social mechanisms to make the technology available and the will to create and use social mechanisms will exist. Physicians, nurses, health care workers, teachers, public and private agencies, and others must see that appropriate equipment is provided.

It was only after they had become sufficiently inexpensive that microcomputers became interesting for people with disabilities. Making them even cheaper and more masterful only enhances the attraction.

Expect advances in user-friendliness. If people with disabilities make their requirements known to the industry, expect user-friendly and less expensive machines to the advantage of users with disabilities.

There are many old people in this country, and there will be more in the future. Old people are more likely than their children to have disabilities. And some old people can use assistance with sequential thought, short-term memory, scheduling appointments, accessing and analyzing databases through a user-friendly interface, and other applications of personal computers that have not yet been explored with regard to their needs.

Environmental control is a key issue to many people with disabilities. Environmental control allows one to turn on the lights, adjust the volume and channel of the television set, activate an emergency message on the phone, and do other useful things. In the future, it will be possible to control ever more of one's house with a personal computer.

Contact will be enhanced not only with the world fashioned by people of the future, but also with worlds not fashioned by people. As an example, there are guidance systems that allow cruise missiles to fly with accuracy. Such guidance systems make it reasonable to suspect that computers will be able to assist many people with disabilities to drive cars.

Robotics is constantly improving. Before the year 2000, probably, robots will be used in special circumstances, and at relatively high expense, for people with disabilities. In the more distant future, the implications of robotics for some people with disabilities are profound.

The future of the interaction of disabled people with their environments through computing technology is promising. Surely something will be done independently by many people with disabilities, and by their allies and their friends. However, coordinated nationwide advocacy would greatly enhance the production of technology and the distribution of it to those who are to benefit.

Social will, social intent, and social promise are not givens. There is an inertia built into existing practice. Teachers do not like to change how they teach, counselors how they counsel, disabled people how they work, disabled students how they learn, and so on. Further, the sort of change involved with computers is disruptive, often with steep learning curves.

Learning about computers is not easy. The school system has been wrestling for some time with the problem of how and what to teach. Industries change their workers' behavior through the incentive of discipline. Acquiring computer skills isolated from an industrial setting for many disabled people involves a learning process that at first may go very slowly. People with disabilities may question whether the eventual payoff will make life that much easier.

Organizations, public and private, concerned with computing and disability are proliferating (see the numerous appendices to this book). Corporations may put disability concerns not on the fringes of American society, but at its center. In our market society, to insulate disabled people from the market is to insulate them from many of the opportunities and responsibilities that other citizens enjoy (and sometimes resent!). But corporate activity in our mixed economy does not preclude the action of the public sector. Traditionally, the two work together in well established ways.

Public Law 94-142, The Education for All Handicapped Children Act, mandates a public education for disabled children. Computing has penetrated other parts of the curriculum. The cultivation of the K–12 market by Apple, IBM, and others has led to a situation where the public school system is increasingly a computer environment. Not to allow students with disabilities full access to this environment is against the intent of 94-142. Whether or not it is strictly against that law awaits the decisions of committees on the handicapped, local education agencies, state education agencies, and ultimately the courts. It would be well if, before the courts ever had to decide such an issue, personal computers for students with disabilities were firmly entrenched in the school system. But the courts may have to decide the relevance of 94-142 to the new computer environments.

Section 504 of the Rehabilitation Act of 1973 is a civil rights act for people with disabilities providing, among other things, that "otherwise qualified handicapped individuals" be provided with "reasonable accommodation." The very definition of reasonable accommodation changes with the existence of computer environments that are more reasonably changeable, more malleable, more accommodative. The number of people disabled but otherwise qualified increases in a world of personal computers. Hopefully, matters will have been facilitated before the courts issue a decision regarding the issue.

The Federal government has been active in funding demonstration projects, centers, and programs. Section 508 of the Rehabilitation Act of 1986 is legislation that would make computers purchased by the Federal government more accessible to people with disabilities. Since the Federal government is the world's largest purchaser of computers, one can expect that computer manufacturers may well make their products usable or adaptable by people with disabilities. This legislation is far reaching. Unfortunately, this law has not received the attention that it merits.

Much remains to be done. Although the efforts mentioned above are significant, they pale next to other possible commitments on the local, state, and national levels and corporate and personal commitments. Whether these commitments will grow is a question that ought to concern people with disabilities, their allies, and their friends, as well as a society that believes in justice, and corporations that believe it is good business to cultivate markets.

Disabilities
and Computers

Computers do not recognize disabilities, as humans do everyday. Much less do they recognize changes from one bureaucracy to the next. The word "disability" means one thing in medicine, another in school, another in vocational rehabilitation, another in civil rights law, another in worker's compensation, and so on. And the terminology changes from time to time and may be different in different countries, and in different social segments of our own country.

In the future it is conceivable that new sophisticated computers and software might exist that, perhaps with video input and the plethora of records that exist around any disabled person, might be able to make the sorts of distinctions indicated above. Such computers could perhaps be programmed for discrimination and even bigotry. The computers of today are incapable of prejudice. That computers today are this stupid makes them less adequate servers of disabilities than they might be. Hopefully when they are smarter they will not be programmed to make prejudiced and bureaucratic judgments about disabilities, but used to serve instead of to know and dominate.

The personal computer can be thought of as interacting with people by input, throughput, and output. These much abused words have a pointed use in relationships with disabilities. Input corresponds roughly to motor disabilities. Throughput corresponds roughly to cognitive disabilities. Output corresponds roughly to sensory disabilities. The three may exist in various combinations.

The rough correspondence will be pursued now as it affects input disability. (Regarding "motor disability," let me repeat that this is a social concept of the relationship between person and environment. Further investigation is needless because of the straightforward concept of input disability, which is all that computers "care" about anyway.) For example, suppose the only input device is a keyboard. This is disabling if the person does not type adequately. This may be because the person never learned to type. This may make an able bodied person disabled in relationship to certain applications of the computer. It may be remedied by learning how to type. If the person has the use of only one finger, no amount of learning will make easy inputs requiring the simultaneous depression of more than one key.

Think of the CONTROL + ALT + DELETE keystroke combination necessary to reboot *MS-DOS* computers. This is purposely difficult because we do not want to reboot computers inadvertently. Yet "difficulty" may become "impossibility" for the user with one finger, a mouth stick, a head pointer, or sometimes one hand.

A useful experiment is to use your personal computer sitting on one hand and making a fist with the other with only the forefinger extended, or, if you want to be more realistic, try your pinky or ring finger. Engineers working on the Apple Macintosh spent a few days doing this and otherwise temporarily disabling themselves. The result of this regarding input disabilities is the Macintosh's *Easy Access* utilities feature that allows the user to depress in sequence keys that would otherwise have to be depressed in concert.

Over half a dozen software packages in the MS-DOS environment allow the same thing. These include *SuperKey, ProKey, PRD +, Filch,* and, most inexpensively, *AccessDOS* shareware from Trace Research and Development Center (Waisman Center and Department of Industrial Engineering, University of Wisconsin, Madison).

SuperKey and *ProKey* have another feature that may be useful to people with input disabilities. It is possible to rearrange the keyboard to your convenience. And what may be merely convenient for an able bodied user may be indispensable for a user with a disability.

For most motor disabilities (input disabilities), changes that make a personal computer accessible are inexpensive and do not disable computers for use by colleagues.

Many other features on a personal computer makes the computer itself remarkably suitable to people with input disabilities. For example, the BACKSPACE/DELETE key eliminates mistakes, as traditionally understood. Even people with input disabilities who can write may find it difficult to erase. The ease of erasing and otherwise correcting mistakes (for instance with the spelling checker) or of preventing mistakes (a spreadsheet has neatness built into it) are boons for many input disabled users.

There are features that should be givens. Modern hard disks are cheap. They are convenient for most people with input disabilities and indispensable for some. Why have floppies to insert and lose if the user can just depress a key? Many users should be insulated from the operating system by a system of icons or a menu. Why type if you can click with a track ball or mouse or if you can just type a single letter?

Note that many people with input disabilities may have difficulty with the mouse. They may prefer a trackball, a mouse worn on the head so that the user has only to look and click, or they may prefer a keyboard. Rule: Different strokes for different folks! Another rule: When considering disabilities there is an exception to every rule. Exceptions can be found by a thorough examination of the possibilities with the disabled user.

Low tech has its place, and frequently the place is invaluable and not to be usurped by high tech. For example, a pencil, eraser down, held in each fist may, for certain people, make for more accuracy when striking the keyboard. Pencils can be found anywhere, no small advantage. Other people may require a head pointer, mouth stick, or simply a pencil held in the teeth to depress the keys on the keyboard. Low tech solutions can be elegant.

Seating and positioning of the keyboard should be considered. And *VGA* may be more comfortable than *CGA*. A small cursor may be hard to catch with a moving head, the cursor enlarging ability of several utilities (Ken Skier's *No-Squint Cursor Enhancer* is robust) may be useful. The person may wish the cursor to travel at a different speed. *Cruise Control* and *Repeat Performance* allow for variations in the speed of the cursor that may be useful.

In addition to keyboard serialization (one finger), *AccessDOS,* from Trace Research and Development Center and distributed free by IBM, contains features that prevent mistakes that some people with motor disabilities are likely to make. For example, it guards against strings like "eeeeee" and against hitting the wrong letter on the way to the right letter. *AccessDOS* is a software approximation to a keyguard (an old favorite) and can often replace it.

A sometime myth holds that a person with a disability can likely be a word processor. While word processing may be a vast improvement over typing and writing, particularly for a person with a disability, it is the most arduous task on a computer that people with input disabilities may face. This is because of the high ratio of input strokes per thought. An art in matching a person with a disability to a personal computer may lie in thinking up tasks that minimize this ratio.

People with more severe input disabilities may require more creative solutions. Since all that is required to interact with a digital computer is the ability to distinguish yes from no, there is, in principle, no reason that anyone with a motor disability should not be able to interact with her or his computer.

Some more challenging instances require a scanner with the person clicking on the correct letter. Such scanners are frequently coupled with rudimentary lexical prediction. Thus, if you choose the letter "b," a list of words beginning with b will appear. When the right one is designated you choose it. If the right one is not in the list, you can spell out the word. Master physicist Stephen Hawking uses such a device (his developed by *Words +*) to talk and to write.

With some people with input disabilities, speech may be difficult to produce or understand. The problem of augmentative communication and of computer use are largely the same. With augmentative communication you use a speech synthesizer. Speech synthesis is the capability of moving from digitized output to speech and exists in many forms, the most elaborate of which is *DECtalk*.

Speech input is a more complex problem. Its attraction for so many insures that intense work experimental and developmental goes on. Currently, an advanced system is produced by Dragon Systems, Inc. Its vocabulary is 30,000 words. It requires a fast 30386 microprocessor, eight megabytes of RAM, and cost $9000 in 1992. Yet there are people for whom such a solution might be necessary, and more for whom it might be optimal.

Inexpensive speech input devices are occasionally useful. If a speech input device can recognize the letters of the alphabet and the rest of the computer keyboard it suffices as an input device.

Speech input raises a question relevant to most computing technology. We know that what is available today will be better in a few years, and that what is not available today may well be available in a few years. Given that, when does one buy what? The answer to this question is pretty much the same as with other computer equipment, except that there is more urgency in providing a first personal computer to a person with a disability.

There are a few people for whom none of the above solutions will work and a few people who specialize in challenging solutions like John Eulenberg of Michigan State. Yet technology moves quickly. What is difficult today may be simple in five years; what seems impossible may become merely difficult.

Or at least so the developers of technology would have it. The problems that people with input disabilities face are not simply technological. They include all the subtle and blatant ways that society discriminates against them. There is little reason to be sanguine that appropriate technology will be appropriately delivered. The sad truth is that entrepreneurship, organization, bureaucracy, education, and policies of the public and private sectors, etc., usually lag behind technology.

This lag may be an opportunity. We are used to imagining a computer as an impersonal agent of change. This perception may be of use with people with disabilities. We can reorganize our educational system and parts of our economic system on the coat tails of computing technology. Our task is to seize the possibility and make it fact.

Important to a person with a disability are the adaptive devices that may be necessary to match her or him to a computer. These may dictate the choice of a computer. Usually there can be no reason to compromise here. An adaptive device can spell the difference between access and no access to a personal computer.

Although the Apple II series has been superseded in power-for-the-penny, it remains dominant in many K–12 school systems. Further, there has been generation of adaptive devices designed around it. Only the brave will select another machine in such K–12 environments. Often, it pays to be brave. Some peripherals are likely to be more expensive for the Apple II.

Often, one ought to consider Macintoshes. Their operating interface is elegant. Many people simply find them easier to use. For a person with a learning disability the icon interface may be a crucial difference. If the only modifications needed come built into the Mac, it becomes a yet more worthy consideration.

Some people with input disabilities are likely to find the mouse used to drive the Macintosh frustrating or impossible to use. Some such people may use a trackball or head mouse. Others do better with a machine not based on mice or their impersonators. Further, Macintosh's are more expensive than many MS-DOS machines.

MS-DOS machines come with various degrees of power. They have the largest software base. A 8088 or 8086 with monochrome monitor and hard disk might be a low end solution and 80386SX with hard disk and VGA monitor is a more deluxe, solution.

The more deluxe solution is often the necessary one. Of course, all the solutions mentioned in this chapter are subject to rapid change. Such change occurs to some extent as a consequence of changes in adaptive technology; yet more, as a consequence of changes in general computer technology. Although hardware is rapidly becoming less expensive, the price of software remains more constant, and the price of labor is increasing. These factors may argue for a more expensive hardware solution than otherwise contemplated.

What about other excellent platforms such as Atari and Commodore Amiga? These often have more power at less cost than counterparts in Macintosh and MS-DOS. Yet they have a less extensive software base, are less likely to be used by others on the job, and are less likely to have adaptive devices made for them. Be warned. But if you are sure they are appropriate do not be deterred.

There are two reasons that a person with a disability ought to have a personal computer. The first is that the world is increasingly accessible through computers. Not being able to use a computer is already starting to be a significant disability in itself. The second is that a personal computer is likely to give a person with a disability an edge. It is a great equalizer.

There is a difference between motor disability and input disability. A paraplegic who is a wheelchair rider has no input disability though she has a motor disability. People like this mar the tidiness of classifications. Mobility may be compromised for such people. They can use computers for telecommunications that increasingly make mobility less necessary than it was. Of course, mobility is a good thing by itself. Going places and doing things help give meaning to a day. But as a means toward an end, it is becoming less necessary.

Allow me to look into the crystal ball. No one can foretell the future unless they control it. Controlling the future makes forecasting as trivial as picking the winner in an athletic event that has been fixed. I shall indulge in two scenarios that are not mutually exclusive.

The first scenario is of the robot. Robots do not have to walk on feet and otherwise mimic the human body. Robots are machines that exert power in the world and are connected to computers. Already robots help build our automobiles and assist in some surgery. There are armlike attachments to wheelchairs that allow quadriplegics to control more of their world. In accomplished versions robots may substitute for human assistants. This makes the disabled person less dependent on others — in short, more independent.

The second scenario is of the six million dollar man. Here various artificial parts are substituted for malfunctioning ones in order to rebuild a human being. We have partial examples of this today from artificial joints to artificial hearts to silicon implants. The logical extension of this technology is to guarantee immortality on earth.

Such technology is fearfully expensive. In addition to not working well, artificial hearts are costly. This technology currently works well only with the simplest of replacements, such as joints, pacemakers, and valves.

Given its relative cheapness, service to people, and mortality, robotic technology is unobjectionable. It promises much benefit to people with disabilities, and thus to society. The technology of the "cyborg" (a human physiologically linked to machinery) is another matter. The social, political, and ethical concerns that attend this technology are obvious and must be dealt with before embarking.

Another part of this technology is of particular relevance to people with disabilities. Disabilities occur in a social context, which, among other things, patronizes, stigmatizes, and oppresses. The message of cyborg technology in this context is clear: Get rid of the social problem of disability by, and only by, getting rid of disability. It promises to eradicate disability independently of social change. Disability need distress no more, since disability is eradicated. . . This vision should not deter us from the near-future benefits of robotic technology serving people with disabilities.

In relation to the computer, some disabilities are of the "throughput" variety. It is tempting to see processes that occur in the computer as occurring in the person. Doing so, we might speak of disabilities in processing, in memory, etc. We must not too readily use the language of computing to describe the minds of people, able-bodied or disabled, yet, we must be open to the possibility that the more complex computers may give us insight into how the human mind works. Perhaps modeling the human mind with the use of artificial intelligence, and using the results to assist the human, we may intervene in a salutary way in throughput disabilities.

Throughput disabilities are complex, intriguing, and among the last disabilities to be assisted by computing. This is ironic. One might expect a computer could straightforwardly substitute for the human mind. To think so would be to suppose that computers are like the human mind. Not yet, if ever.

People with disabilities are as complex and varied as all other people. Throughput disabilities may have to do with retardation, itself misunderstood and complex. As it is socially constructed, intelligence is multifaceted; by extension, retardation must be multifaceted.

As for learning disabilities, one strand of research suggests that a "learning disability" is "retardation" when it happens in a poor person; another maintains that it is a tag to deal with people who are not retarded but who are not well reached by the school system. There are disabilities from dyslexia to dysgraphia that are connected with illiteracy and innumeracy. Other forms of learning disabilities may involve differences in pathways that bring information to the brain. Other learning disabilities may involve the perception of loud background noise. There are many more.

In some cases, learning disabilities may be throughput disabilities, although more generally they may be thought of as representing input or output disabilities. For instance, a person's difficulty with typing may be the result of a learning disability, as may be a difficulty in decoding what appears on the screen. In general, throughput disabilities present themselves as complex interactions of input, throughput, and output disabilities. At this stage of our knowledge, the most useful approaches avoid any sort of theories in the application of computer capabilities to people with throughput disabilities. Some examples follow.

We know enough about people to know that a rebuff by a teacher may be painful to the person rebuffed, and perhaps to the teacher. What if mistakes are pointed out by a computer, say by a corrective beep or by the absence of a new graphical reward? These mistakes, learned about in private, do not become a social issue to compound the difficulties of a disabled person.

It seems reasonable to have personal computers take over parts of the education of people with throughput disabilities. Yet it should not be thought that people with throughput disabilities need a teacher less than other people. It would be a tragic outcome if computing were to lead to the consignment of people with throughput disabilities to a special classroom where personal computers took over from teachers.

We know that some people like to have letters enlarged. Other people like to be read to. The arsenal of adaptive equipment that has proved so beneficial to people who are visually impaired seems unusually valuable to some people with throughput disabilities.

Software programs that involve lexical predictions appear to ease writing for some. The task of writing frequently becomes one of choosing among several possible words. In some sense, it appears that to write becomes to read. Sometimes the correct word does not even have to be presented. It appears that something like the hesitancy of the stutter or the Parkinsonian gait is involved. What may be required is getting the person started and restarted. Lexical prediction appears to have a role with some people with throughput disabilities.

Touch screens, sometimes appear beneficial. The interface on the Macintosh or with Microsoft's Windows may have significant benefit for some people with some throughput disabilities. Operating such interfaces requires a mouse, or other pointing device, and a clicker. It may be that this works better than a keyboard for people with some learning disabilities as well as some people who are retarded.

What about calculators? We normally do not want calculators used until students know something about operations with pencil and paper (if they can use pencil and paper). But at what age, for what people, with what disabilities?

The same with spelling checkers. There are many able-bodied people who are simply poor spellers, and an education spent rectifying their spelling weakness may be counterproductive not only in time but with the rest of the curriculum. What about people with learning disabilities or who are retarded? At some time in life they perhaps should use spelling checkers. When, for who, in what way?

A rough and ready empiricism may go some way for people with throughput disabilities. Still, a more detailed program of research is needed; the benefits are incalculable.

There are smart and foolish ways of using computers in a classroom. It is important that they be used to improve the learning of the child first and the appearance of the work second. For example, using word processors to copy a draft laboriously produced with paper and pencil is to misuse them. This holds for children with disabilities.

The relationship of a student with a throughput disability to a computer can be one of privacy. Computers don't shout what a student is doing to the rest of the class, nor even to the teacher. This may make the student try things she ordinarily wouldn't, and may preserve her self esteem. Risk taking and self-confidence are taken out of many students and probably more students with disabilities, including throughput disabilities.

Personal computers are "patient." Indeed, this very human word doesn't really apply. Computers simply don't care about having to repeat things, nor do they care if it takes a while before an input. In some settings computers are programmed to care. Still, impatience is not the rule. The reliability computers show is often a virtue; being patiently reliable — steadfast — is a double virtue.

You may have noticed that time seems to change with some activities on a computer. You may play computer games. Children you know may be Nintendo addicts or arcade maniacs. Computers can be catchy. Software can be written to be catchy. This may be useful for some children with various throughput disabilities.

Able-bodied people grow up manipulating the furniture of their world. A body of anecdotal and formal evidence suggests that this may be necessary for development in thought. It may also be necessary for emotional development. Children with some disabilities may find it difficult to manipulate their physical world. It may be easier to manipulate a computer world.

There are indications that computer worlds can be designed so as to foster intellectual and emotional growth. Used correctly that is a purpose of *LOGO*, for example. This is relevant to people with throughput disabilities. It is relevant to education. Details of software may not be worked out for many children, yet this is reason enough to make personal computers appropriate. Here is an important and fruitful research agenda that is only barely begun.

Finally, we come to output disabilities. These include varying degrees of visual impairment. A person may not be able to see the screen; the screen may be blurred; the letters may be too small. Always the person's ability to decode output of the monitor is compromised. As the monitor screen is the standard means of temporary output to the person (printed copy is more permanent, magnetic disks are unintelligible to people), this makes the computer unusable except if the person is a perfect touch typist and can perfectly trust that she is typing what she thinks she is typing. Such people do not exist. Everyone needs some verification; everyone needs feedback.

The notion of feedback is worth a few words. It grew in two movements. The first movement attached to the growth in computing itself. The second movement infiltrated jargon. Here feedback had a confused role. Positive feedback was vaguely good, negative feedback bad. In fact, negative feedback used information from the output, reversed its sign, and fed it to the input. Thus does a thermostat sense the temperature of a room and feed it back negatively to the furnace. Room too hot — furnace off; room too cold — furnace on.

Negative feedback is critical to the control of artifacts from guided missiles to computers and computer-person systems. If the person is disabled from decoding the output, impossible perfection is demanded or chaos follows. Changing the outputs, we can often restore a working system.

The stereotype of the young blind adult, German shepherd in hand, playing the piano, and studiously reading braille, is an image that we would do well to change. Labrador retrievers are gaining in popularity. Blind people are not all musical. The majority of blind people do not read braille. Most blindness and visual impairment occurs in people over the age of sixty-five. Blind people are not a homogeneous group.

Most people who have visual impairments can see something. What they see may be blurred, or restricted to the center of their field of vision, or cause undue strain, etc. Perhaps these or other problems are solved by enlarging the video display. Expensive solutions include large monitors.

More inexpensive are solutions that magnify an area of an ordinary display. Typically, such solutions allow for variation in size, the ability to move the magnified area around the display, locate the cursor, and switch back and forth from enlarged screen to unmodified screen. These abilities come as software or hardware. Some are free; many are of moderate price, some are expensive. Often, they are combined with devices that magnify the printed page. The combination allows many people with visual impairments to become proficient secretaries. This leads to the misunderstanding that this is a desirable vocation for most with limited vision, the possibility demanding the fact. Is this a proper logic of technology?

Should vision not be useful for decoding visual output on a computer, there are other options. Braille printers exist. These do not provide the immediate feedback necessary to using a computer. Nonetheless, they can be used for long term feedback on projects.

For immediate feedback other devices exist. Voice output works elegantly for many blind persons. It has two parts. One part, hardware, transforms the output of a computer into output that drives a loudspeaker. The other part, frequently software, sends the appropriate output from the computer to the first part. These screen readers allow one to read the last word typed, a sentence, the full document, and so on.

The price of voice transducers roughly depends on the quality of the voice and is between $100 and $5000. A nonvocal person wishing a transducer to speak for her might be properly disturbed at sounding like a robot. Many blind people don't care, needing only a transducer that they can understand. Such a transducer is likely to cost less than $500, which is also about the price for some typical screen readers.

Suitably equipped, personal computers can talk. Suitably trained, blind people can use talking computers.

Coupled with suitable applications software, talking computers can do more than is obvious. For example, computers can search databases electronically and then give the results as speech — no need to listen to everything in between. Some people of limited vision may do best with a combination of a talking computer and screen enlargement.

Intelligent scanners can read text. This can be converted into speech. This output also can be sent to a computer for storage, to be played back later. Thus material from conventional libraries (and offices) can be made accessible to people who cannot read. As libraries become more electronic this conversion process will be less necessary, it being necessary only to transform electronic media into speech.

Equipped with appropriately modified computers, blind and visually impaired people find an array of significant life activities accessible. Personal computers can make a decisive difference.

Moving

Matching a person with a disability with an appropriate personal computer is often fairly simple. If an appropriate computer match results in greater quality of life, independence, employability, income — computers pay off. They can be appropriate from early childhood to special education to vocational rehabilitation to the work force to retirement.

Many private sector firms adopting computers count only about 40 percent of computer expenses in hardware and software. The other 60 percent is in training people. Not surprisingly, most of the cost in appropriate computers for people with disabilities is in their training. These training costs are often overlooked.

The costs are as low as 60 percent in the private sector because the choice is often one of compute or move on. Similar incentives for those in the educational or rehabilitation system may not exist. They should not exist.

Teaching computing skills should be coupled with teaching dignity, responsibility, and independence to the person with a disability. Computing is not enough. But personal computers are a splendid fulcrum around which to leverage other parts of the education and training of people with disabilities. Matching an appropriate computer is but the first step in a process involving education, training, motivation, self-confidence, aspiration, risk-taking. Leverage, always leverage.

I sketched earlier some of what is possible with a word processor. I suggested that word processors are an enormous improvement over typewriters and pens for able-bodied and disabled people alike. I pointed to some particular uses and advantages for people with disabilities. However, there is a danger.

Although word processing is dandy for everyone, disabled and able-bodied, and is more often necessary for people who are disabled, it ought not be the goal of everyone with a disability. Except in cases of interest, proclivity, or job word processing may well not be optimal. A narrow eye on word processing trims the sails of the person with a disability and neglects other possibilities that may be more interesting, appealing, and lucrative.

Education in the use of computers should be coupled with general changes in educational practice in prekindergarten through high school, college, graduate, vocational, and professional education. The challenge of education and computers has scarcely been met; the insertion of appropriate computing for people with disabilities into educational curricula has scarcely begun. Education about computers for people with disabilities can lead the way in changing education for all.

In what follows, I will sketch some of what can be done in education and after with personal computers. These sketches are hardly complete. And there is no one-to-one relation between them and jobs. Sometimes, they are sketches of the center of jobs. Yet a job always requires more. And much more can be done with personal computers than I talk about here. In the future, there will be still more.

The modern digital computer executes an often lengthy series of simple instructions. These instructions are either given to the computer in "machine language" or in a variety of "high level" languages with names such as *Fortran, COBOL, BASIC, Pascal, LISP, LOGO, APL, C + +*. Computer programming is rule governed, putting small pieces together into a larger whole according to rules.

Despite the fact that computer languages and the languages that people naturally speak are both called languages, they should not be confused. That rules profoundly govern the deep structure of natural languages has become a seriously arguable point only recently. Computing languages are rule governed by design.

Compared to natural language, computer languages are parsimonious or terse. It requires thought to write a program. For people with difficulties in typing or other modes of inputting and with the aptitude to think in the algorithmic ways of computer languages, a job in programming may be attractive. Such jobs have the further advantage that in most colleges and universities there are well defined studies that lead to proficiency in them.

But one does not have to be a programmer to use a computer. In the future running a computer will be easier, a function of programming that will make programming and computing seem ever further apart. Yet programming is a viable option for some people with disabilities. Barriers to it include the often dismal mathematical and scientific education many people with disabilities receive in the K–12 system.

In primary and secondary schools, programming, where it exists, often starts with the bare rudiments of *LOGO,* which at the simple level is a complex way to draw simple figures. After this introduction to how a computer can make life harder, students proceed to *BASIC,* a usually outdated language designed for machines when memory was expensive.

Such a sequence in the K–12 curriculum ought to be replaced by an introduction to *LOGO* that captures the ability of that language not only to make simple drawing difficult but to make difficult drawing simple, and complex procedures perspicuous. *LOGO* is more than a language to draw pictures. This might be followed by *Pascal.* In high school, this might be followed by *C + +,* a language that promises to be significant in the 90s.

But changes in teaching are not easy. They involve teaching teachers languages that they may not know, and teaching the teachers of other subjects (such as mathematics, sciences, English) the relevance of computing to their subjects — a tall order. A need for fluency with computers has been imposed upon us as much as anything by international competition. It is part of the general improvement of the American educational system recognized to be a necessity as we enter the next century. Would it not be splendid if special education were to point the way toward the realization of it?

Programming also should be investigated at the college, university, and graduate level. It is not too late to learn here. People with disabilities who enter college may benefit from it as a major and as a future focus of income-producing labor. More people with disabilities than those who have majored in computer science could benefit from the major.

Software packages are becoming more complex to the computer and more simple and powerful to the user. Let me return to other sketches of what appropriate adaptive computing hardware and software can do when coupled with such packages.

From time to time, we all use databases. The database might be a phone book that contains the names and telephone numbers of all people within a specified geographical area who have telephones and have not chosen to have unlisted numbers. The rules for looking up a telephone number are simple, provided that the user of the directory is literate, knows how to sort through names by alphabetical order, and knows the last name and the first name, or at least has a good idea of the first name.

If, however, I am interested in having my refrigerator repaired, reading through a whole telephone book in order to find the name of the refrigerator repairperson is tedious and probably unproductive. I may ask either a friend or acquaintance for the name of a refrigerator repairperson and look up the number, or I may turn to the yellow pages and look under "Refrigerator, Repair." In looking for "Refrigerator," I could be directed toward "Appliances."

What if my son has gone out the back door, he is late, dinner is about to reach the table, and I know he has gone to Mike's house, Mike being the name of the father of my son's friend, and Mike's house is on Jay Street between Dove and Swan streets but closer to Dove Street across the street from the back door of my house. Although I may have sufficient information to find the phone number in the white pages, by the time I do find it dinner is likely to be cold. The rational procedure in this case is to go out the door to the house that I know to be Mike's, ring the bell, and ask for my son.

It might be possible to arrange a telephone directory that would permit me to find Mike's phone number. It is possible to find phone numbers according to a variety of criteria. But it does not pay the telephone company to print up a separate directory for most needs.

Many other databases exist. The Department of Motor Vehicles has vehicle registration numbers, driver's license numbers, and other items. This information is broken into separate listings constructed so they form, in the language of databases, "fields." One field may be last names, another field license numbers, and so on.

Databases exist all around us. It is possible to connect databases — the Internal Revenue Service information on one, one's medical data, employment record, insurance situations, credit ratings, mail-order buying habits, convictions or other legal matters — into a collection of searchable databases. Were this to happen, one's privacy would just about disappear. Herein is a danger of computers worth noting.

The manipulation of databases is often useful. Databases organized in certain ways can form management information systems. Manipulating such systems is an important activity of modern life. Computers make large databases manipulable and possible. Finding the needle in the haystack is a function of access to the database.

Databases can be accessible through computers. People with disabilities can use them if they can use computers. A person who cannot use a computer is disabled as regards many databases. Many jobs involve the manipulation of databases.

For example, a journalist contemplates writing an article that requires going through various databases to pick out relevant information. To make searches easier, databases routinely send requests for summaries to authors of articles. If the journalist is visually impaired, she or he will be able to conduct a search only having to read, or have the computer read out, the names or abstracts of the relevant articles.

Of interest to people with disabilities are databases called Personal Information Managers. Easy to use and typically only by the interested person, such databases ordinarily have the characteristic that the volume of information is relatively small. This sort of database may even partially substitute for memory in people with certain kinds of impairments.

How would it be for us to have everything that we ever wrote in our own database accessible to us even if we forgot it? (Yet perhaps some forgetfulness is essential to novelty.)

Various databases are becoming more integral to various jobs. Insofar as a job is concerned with databases, it is open and accessible to a person with a disability, provided the person has access to an appropriate computer.

One version of the history of personal computers claims that software started the personal computer race. *VisiCalc,* a software spread sheet, allowed for budgets, business plans, and other complex numerical relationships to be calculated and recalculated flexibly and easily. This electronic ledger made the Apple as important to business as it has become in the K–12 classroom. Up went the sales of the Apple. *VisiCalc* was later superseded by *Lotus 1-2-3, Excel,* and *Quattro Pro* spreadsheets — electronic ledgers on increasingly powerful hardware platforms.

Neatness is designed in, handy for some with disabilities: a spread–sheet has rows and columns. Each cell can be identified by its coordinates. For example, "B7" is the cell which is the second over and the seventh down. Each cell can accept words or numbers. The cells can have defined mathematical relationships to various other cells. Thus, for example, if I change a quantity in one cell, automatically the other cells dependent on it are recalculated.

Spreadsheets may be valuable to certain jobs. If these jobs are performed on computers accessible to people with disabilities, the jobs are available to them. Here again, a wide array of jobs once closed to persons with disabilities is opened.

There is more specialized software. It is possible and often necessary to use a computer to do accounting, making the accounting profession accessible to people with disabilities who have access to a computer. Such people can work for corporations, accounting firms, or themselves. Using modems and telecommunication software they may be able to do substantial parts of their jobs from their homes.

Unfortunately, accounting is usually taught with the introductory courses in pen and pencil on a neatly laid-out page, exactly the sort of combination that may be difficult for a person with a disability. The problem is revising the curriculum.

Personal computers with spreadsheets often have distributed the tasks accomplishable by spreadsheets throughout organizations rather than with one person. In so doing, computing has redefined jobs. New jobs may well be accessible to a person with disabilities to an extent that earlier jobs were not.

Recently changed jobs will change again and again in the future. The person with a disability must not only be trained to do one job with a computer but must be educated in the use of computers and to an openness toward new hardware and software.

Systems for the manipulation of numbers, databases, etc., make domains once accessible to the typewriter, pen or pencil accessible by computer, and accessibility is to the benefit of people with disabilities.

Computer Assisted Design is used in architecture, landscape architecture, aeronautics, and many other endeavors and even in the design of computers and computer chips. Computer Assisted Design makes use of the accessibility to people of visual images. Visualization requires accuracy, rotation in three dimensions, and manipulations of various sorts, and makes heavy demands on the computer, on the software, and initially on the pocketbook; it is expensive to buy the software, laser printers, plotters, and high resolution monitors and display subsystems.

Computer Assisted Design is used in the education of people with disabilities. Valencia Community College (in Orlando, Florida) and the Maryland Rehabilitation Center (in Baltimore), have constructed training programs around CAD, assuming the high expense in capital justifies large investments in labor. The outcome is disabled people who are able to enter the job market often with special skills.

With some of the features of CAD and some of the features of word processors, another entry into the workplace is desk-top publishing. With desk-top publishing you can do things like change size and type faces, break text up into columns, add pictures, drawings, and diagrams perhaps with the computer, have words go round in circles or slide off the page aslant.

Desk-top publishing is useful in large organizations and corporations, for communications between organizations, and for communications to other people. Producing a professional-looking newsletter is possible with desk-top publishing. Desk-top publishing creates new jobs, redistributes old ones, and makes these jobs accessible to people with a computer and hence to people with disabilities.

Art, such as the creation of music or visual images, once frequently inaccessible to people with disabilities, is now accessible to those who have computers. There are many other uses for computers. In the future there will be more.

It is now often possible for a set of unconnected activities that can be performed by a person with a disability to be manipulated together into a productive job. By renegotiating the character of tasks, jobs, work, and the career ladder the computer has made it possible to reach certain kinds of jobs in many ways other than the traditional ones. Flexibility in the job market is good for people with disabilities.

Going

Personal computers can have a grand effect on the lives of people with disabilities. They can for example alter work, what constitutes a job, what the organization of work looks like, where the job is done, whether the job can be done by a person with a disability, and so on. By now the technology is sufficiently inexpensive to be available to all. Where special adaptations are required, they usually exist.

Work is central. It defines a person in society. Not to have a job is to be stigmatized. If a person does not have a job out of preference, he or she is considered criminal, lazy, promiscuous. It is often thought that not having a job because one is unable to work is more honorable. But even in cases where not being able to work seems to carry with it no penalties, it often does. Military service may appear honorable but often has associated with it distortions in the job ladder. Childbirth is only a temporary excuse. An acute disease is acute for only so long. Despite civility and law, there are penalties to pay for not working.

People with disabilities may be among the "worthy poor," people who can't work for physical or health reasons beyond their control. But many people with disabilities, however "worthy" and excusable, still want most just to work. Some want to because of an experience of impotence and obsolescence that too often comes with being categorized as part of the worthy poor. Being on the dole is unpleasant no matter how worthy one is. The Americans with Disabilities Act of 1990 and sections 503 and 504 of the Rehabilitation Act of 1973 provide that people with disabilities need not automatically put up with being part of the worthy poor.

The penalties of not working, even if one is part of the worthy poor, are not the only reason for one to want to work. Another reason is that work is almost always the only route to a decent income. A decent income is the main route to adventure and security alike. Although the best things in life may be free, the truth is that life is made up of a collection of second-bests.

74

Work is influential well beyond itself. It justifies serious education. Disabled children who may grow up with scant prospects of a job may be taught differently from children who grow up to be in the future labor force.

Whether work should be central may be debatable. Whether it *is* central is beyond debate.

In the language of economics, the computer acts on the "supply side," increasing the "human capital" that the person with a disability brings to the labor market. In everyday language, the person with a disability often has more to offer with a computer.

Still, having more to offer is insufficient if the labor market discriminates against disabled people. That this is true is well recognized, eventuating in 1990 in the passage of the Americans with Disabilities Act. It is appropriate in this context to quote from the preamble to this landmark legislation overwhelmingly passed by the Congress and signed by the President.

(a) Findings. The Congress finds that

(1) some 43,000,000 Americans have one or more physical or mental disabilities, and this number is increasing as the population as a whole is growing older;

(2) historically, society has tended to isolate and segregate individuals with disabilities, and despite some improvements such forms of discrimination against individuals with disabilities continue to be a serious and pervasive social problem;

(3) discrimination against individuals with disabilities persists in such critical areas as employment, housing, public accommodations, education, transporation, communication, recreation, institutionalization, health services, voting, and access to public services.

(4) unlike individuals who have experienced discrimination on the basis of race, color, sex, national origin, religion or age, individuals who have experienced discrimination on the basis of disability have often had no legal recourse to redress such discrimination;

(5) individuals with disabilities continually encounter various forms of discrimination, including outright intentional exclusion. The discriminatory effects of architectural, transportation, and communication barriers, overprotective rules and policies, failure to make modifications to existing facilities and practice exclusionary qualification standards and criteria, segregation and relegation to lesser services, programs, activities, benefits, jobs or other opportunities;

(6) census data, national polls, and other studies have documented that people with disabilities, as a group, occupy an inferior status in our

society, and are extremely disadvantaged socially, vocationally, economically and educationally;

(7) individuals with disabilities are a discrete and insular minority who have been faced with restrictions and limitations subjected to a history of purposeful, unequal treatment, and relegated to a position of political powerlessness in our society based on characteristics that are beyond the control of such individuals and resulting from stereotypic assumptions not truly indicative of the individual ability of such individuals to participate in and contribute to society;

(8) the Nation's proper goals regarding individuals with disabilities are to assure equality of opportunity, full participation, independent living and economic self-sufficiency for such individuals and

(9) the continuing existence of unfair and unnecessary discrimination and prejudice denies people with disabilities the opportunity to compete on an equal basis and to pursue those goals for which our free society is justifiably famous and costs the United States billions of dollars a year in unnecessary expenses resulting from dependency and productivity.

(b) Purpose. It is the purpose of this Act

(1) to provide a clear and comprehensive national mandate for the elimination of discrimination against individuals with disabilities;

(2) to provide clear, strong, consistent, enforceable standards addressing discrimination against people with disabilities; and

(3) to ensure that the Federal Government plays a central role in enforcing the standards established in this Act on behalf of individuals with disabilities; and

(4) to invoke the sweep of congressional authority, including the power to invoke the fourteenth amendment and to regulate commerce, in order to address the major areas of discrimination faced day-to-day by people with disabilities.

The findings of this act state clearly that people with disabilities are a large American minority that has weathered isolation, segregation, and discrimination. The Americans with Disabilities Act extends and amplifies prior legislation for people with disabilities. It provides for an active role by the federal government. Much of the act concerns employment. To this problem are brought the honed instruments of the American tradition of civil rights.

To traditional members of the worthy poor, to patients taken care of, to people with a social niche to cradle them, being ripped, however timely, from habit is a significant matter. Why would a person with a disability wish to be considered a member of a minority group? In truth, most people with disabilities suffer the discrimination and other social pains of minority group members already. The choice of being treated as a member of a minority group is already made irrespective of the decision of individuals with disabilities.

It is not people with disabilities who make the decision to be a minority group, it is society. Treated as a minority, people with disabilities have gotten it together to protect themselves under law as a minority group. Given the findings of the Congress of the United States above, it is a propitious move.

Generally, the Americans with Disabilities Act affects the demand site of the equations that determine the labor force participation of people with disabilities and increase the payoffs to investments in education, health care, rehabilitation, etc. The Act decreases the costs of supplemental security insurance, social security disability insurance, and the like. Though these considerations of cost efficiency are consequential, they pale next to the enhanced justice, humanity and dignity that are consequences of the Americans with Disabilities Act. Personal computers, of course, affect the supply side of these economic equations. People with disabilities with computers are often more valuable resources than people without disabilities with computers.

Legislation such as the Americans with Disabilities Act that largely affects the demand side enriches the effects of improvements on the supply side. This includes personal computers as explored in this book. Far from making computers gratuitous, the Act makes them all the more important. Simplistically, an enforced Americans with Disabilities Act will create a social and economic environment where people with disabilities will be able to make use of what they have. I hope they will have appropriate computers.

The Americans with Disabilities Act not only holds that people with disabilities constitute a political minority, it assures that this minority will be more powerful in the future. Talking about a minority in federal legislation is not mere talk; it is empowering talk. This empowerment goes well with empowering computing technology. And, people empowered are more likely to gain access to the tools of power including appropriate computing.

The Act extends beyond itself in another sense as well. It is the first major federal legislation fought for (and well) by people with disabilities and their allies. It marks the maturation of the disability rights movement. As is the way with politics, success here enhances the chances of success elsewhere in the political arena. Indeed it marks a new era for people with disabilities where their civil and political rights and efficacy are a force in American politics.

In distinction to the Americans with Disabilities Act, two important earlier acts, while for people with disabilities were not by and of them. These are sections 503 and 504 of the Rehabilitation Act of 1973, and Public Law 94-142, the Education for All Handicapped Children Act, of 1975. Both acts are in the civil rights tradition; 503 and 504 provide significant civil rights for people with disabilities in organizations that receive grants or contracts from the federal government.

Although PL 94-142 is currently implemented largely as service legislation, its original intent was to provide an equal integrated education for children with disabilities. While the language of both acts makes it clear that they were written in the spirit of and by people who knew the American civil rights tradition, people with disabilities did not have a significant role in either act. Although people with disabilities have benefited much from both acts, they were essentially gifts. Still, the gifts were generous and helped a nascent disability rights movement.

Federal legislation is not magic. To work it must be implemented. Part of the implementation is in the regulations of the law. People with disabilities had a substantial role in the adoption of the regulations to 504 which had been passed earlier under the Nixon administration.

President Carter's Secretary of Health, Education and Welfare found disabled people on his lawn one morning, backed up by the media. There were demonstrations by disabled people across the country, including one in San Francisco that saw people with disabilities arrested and taken to jail. The regulations were adopted shortly after. This was a major national victory of people with disabilities acting in the tradition of civil rights.

People with disabilities were involved in another national victory. In the Grove City decision of 1984, the Supreme Court held that only those parts of an organization that directly involved federal contracts or grants were to be held accountable to civil rights enforcement. This included African Americans, women, and people with disabilities. People with disabilities initially led the fight for the Civil Rights Restoration Act, which effectively reversed Grove City.

In part, this leadership had stemmed from a national meeting of disability rights activists and women, blacks, Native Americans, and members of other civil rights groups. In this meeting, organized by the Disability Rights Educational Defense Fund in 1983, connections were made that were to endure. Further, although the Disability Rights Education Defense Fund had initially proposed voting rights for people with disabilities, the discussions in San Francisco anticipated the attacks on civil rights that came and established a Washington branch of the Disability Rights Education Defense Fund charged *inter alia* with preserving 504.

Vice President George Bush headed a commission for regulatory reform. Initially, 503 and 504 were regarded as regulations instead of civil rights mandates. The disability rights movement earned Bush's respect, and later he endorsed the Americans with Disabilities Act.

Legislation directly concerning disability and technology was enacted during the 1980s. The Harkin Act provided for the establishment of state centers for technology. A list of current ones appears here as an appendix.

The Rehabilitation Act of 1986 contained section 508, which holds that electronic office equipment bought by the federal government shall be accessible or shall be readily made accessible to people with disabilities.

Potentially, this is a powerful section. The federal government is the world's single largest purchaser of computers. The additional cost of adaptive modifications designed into computers at the start is small if spread over all computers produced. These two facts argue for changes in future computing equipment for everyone since it usually does not pay manufacturers to sell one set of computers to the government and another set elsewhere.

The combination of propitious legislation and the political coming of age that has distinguished the disability rights movement in the last two decades has changed what it is to be disabled in America. These changes start with the identity of people with disabilities, radiate toward interaction with society, and strike the very roots of the social construction of disability.

As the American Disabilities Act becomes better known through effective enforcement, a culminating change in the social construction of disability may well occur. If changes in society continue as they have, being disabled will be a less painful experience. Necessary pain is lamentable; unnecessary pain is terrible.

As history progresses, technology progresses, partially by scientific logic, partially by social logic, and partially through a logic of its own. Technology has much to offer people with disabilities; will the promise be realized?

The answer is unclear. It is a concern of some that people with disabilities be matched with appropriate computing technology. This is usually straightforward. Further, the resources required are usually small. The organizational capacity is now fairly well assured through public, private, and university centers. State centers issuing from the Harkin act are helping assure adequate matching of appropriate computing technology to people with diverse disabilities. Still, is this cause to be sanguine about the realization of the promise?

I think not. Other significant barriers to appropriate computing exist.

Technology changes. We know it not only because we are told it, but because we see it and feel it. What we had yesterday is obsolete today; what we have today will be obsolete tomorrow. Change is likely to be painful for many people who work for corporations. Still, the change to modern technologies is important for productivity and competitiveness.

Many corporations regularly pay a good deal more for retraining than for new computing technology. The technology can be awkward for corporations and able-bodied people. How is it for people with disabilities? Although the benefits are likely to be greater, there is little reason to expect the awkwardness to be less. It may well be greater. Who is to train the person with a disability in the use of adaptive equipment? Often, it does not suffice only to know about computers. And who shall train the trainers?

Although adaptive technology changes more slowly than computing technology, it changes too. A person with a disability can be well matched, but if technology changes, the appropriate match is likely to change.

There is an important difference between being technologically up to date and having technology that is functionally appropriate. From this derive two arguments. The first has to do with making matches that not only will work with today's adaptive technology but are likely to work with tomorrow's. Try to see that the technology is modular, allowing for the substitution of components that are likely to support future adaptive equipment. Do not believe that you can foretell the future.

The second argument is that a mechanical match is insufficient. The person must be educated to be a good consumer and must be educated to teach herself or himself. The person must be part of a system of information that can be brought to bear as appropriate. This is an appropriate role for organizations such as those funded through the Harkin Act.

People with disabilities are unlikely to be wealthy. Those who are wealthy are best served by keeping abreast of new developments and making new purchases as warranted. Corporations and other employers may be best served by making purchases at the recommendation of a disabled employee. As of 1991 the reasonable accommodation language of federal law had not been applied to computers. There is reason that it should be.

Many people with disabilities have computing technology financed by a third party. While third parties may underwrite the cost of a first computer, particularly if it is required for employment, third parties may be reluctant to fund second and third computers. The vocational rehabilitation system is charged with finding work and with providing the means to work. The working person with a disability must currently often look elsewhere for funds for appropriate computing technology. Even with deft matching, the distance between a person with a disability and an appropriate personal computer may be great.

The employer can provide the computer, with or without the guidance of section 508 of the Rehabilitation Act of 1986, sections 503 and 504 of the Rehabilitation Act of 1973, or the Americans with Disabilities Act.

One possibility is the restructuring of third party payment. If found medically necessary for a given individual, computing technology could be purchased by private and government health insurance. A vocational rehabilitation system concerned with life after placement could fund computing technology for clients with jobs. Technology loan systems, "computer libraries," might be established to keep people up to date with computing technology at what might be a lower cost and a higher level of benefit.

Another possibility is the funding of computing technology by the person with a disability. Tax credits might make this easier.

It is important that these alternatives be integrated and not be isolated. If organizational change is required, it is important not to miss the opportunity to make more decisive change that may well extend beyond computing.

Such changes cannot be left to chance. People with disabilities have often been left to chance, and chance has often been unkind. To leave matters to chance is to lose out on the significant promise of computing technology for people with disabilities and on the even more significant opportunity for organizational change that can attend computing technology.

This book has not primarily been about computing technology used to enhance the efficiency of organizations. Nor has it been about computing technology as a mechanism of domination. It has, I hope, been a book of enablement and empowerment. There is no need to advocate for computing technology to enhance efficiency and increase domination.

It might be thought that people with disabilities would suffer and benefit as much by computing technology used in this way as other people. This is only true insofar as people with disabilities are held equal to other people. As the Congress of the United States found in its Preamble to the Americans with Disabilities Act, they are not always held equal.

If persons with disabilities are at the bottom of the heap, they will disproportionately suffer from the regimentation made possible by computing technology. If, more often than other people, they are clients, patients, or the like, computing technology will be used to keep track of them, treat them as cases not people, and otherwise increase the indignities to which they are subjected. A book on socially vulnerable people and such uses of computing ought to be written. This has not been that book.

We have been talking about the fact that personal computers have an enormous capacity to serve, enable, and empower people with disabilities. In part, this capacity is unique to people with disabilities. For the rest, it is shared with the power that personal computers have to empower everybody. To see that computers benefit people with disabilities will require knowledge and will. This book had tried to sketch some of the knowledge. It will also require will of the sort that propelled the Americans with Disabilities Act into law.

Appendix A:
Selected Product and
Vendor Information

AbiliCAD
AbiliTech
502 N. Davis Ave., P.O. Box 635
Thief River Falls, MN 56701
(617) 577-8500
  Price: $550
  Requires: AutoCAD, Release 10
(MS-DOS)
  In Short: Adds alpha-numeric keys
and calculator as a drop-down menu
choices within *AutoCAD*'s drawing
editor. Compatible with any mouse
emulating device (such as track-balls
or electronic head pointers). Does
not address keyboard (or mouse) access when not in the drawing editor
(or for MS-DOS). Versions are also
available that work well with some
Prentke Romich devices, such as
LightTalker and *TouchTalker.* Only
machine language code (compiled)
menus are readily available, making
further modification of the *AbiliCAD*
(or *AutoCAD*) menus complicated.

AccessDOS **Version 1.0,** *One Finger*
  Version 5.05, *QuicKey* **(discon-**
  tinued)
Trace Research and Development
  Center
Waisman Center and Department of

Industrial Engineering
University of Wisconsin-Madison
S-151 Waisman Center
1500 Highland Ave.
Madison, WI 53705-2280
(608) 262-6922, (608) 263-5408
  Price: All products are distributed
as shareware

Bug Voice Command System
Command Corp., Inc.
3675 Crestwood Pkwy.
Duluth, GA 30136
(404) 925-7950
  Price: $1,195 (DOS Professional)
  Requires: Any MS-DOS CAD system
  In Short: A speech recognition
system specifically designed (and advertised) for use with CAD. Offers
keyboard emulation only. Recognition accuracy is very good, but
limited vocabulary makes hand-free
access to the keyboard (or to a CAD
command menu structure) impractical. No comprehensive starter
vocabulary. Product is not meant
(nor is it advertised) to do anything
but augment the efficiency of a fully
able-bodied (but perhaps clumsy)
ten-fingered typist.
  Several other brands of low-end

speech recognition systems are
available.

DECtalk
Digital Equipment Corporation
Continental Blvd.
Merrimack, NH 03054
(603) 884-8990
Price: $4498

Doug Clapp's Word Tools
Aegis Development
2115 Pico Blvd.
Santa Monica, CA 99405
(213) 392-9972
Price: $79

Dragon Dictate
Ninety Bridge St.
Newton, MA 02158
(617) 965-5200
Price: $9000

Easy Access, ImageWriter II, Macintosh Classic, Macintosh SE/30, Macintosh LC, Macintosh IIsi
Apple Computers Incorporated
20525 Mariani Ave.
Cupertino, CA 95014
(408) 996-1010
Prices: $0 (*Easy Access* — bundled
with System software), $399 (*Image-Writer*), $1180 (*Macintosh Classic*),
$2179 (*SE/30*), $1501 (*LC*), $2453
(*IIsi*)

EyeRelief, Ken Skier's No-Squint Cursor Enhancer
SkiSoft Publishing Corporation
1644 Massachusetts Ave.
Suite 79
Lexington, MA 02173
(800) 662-3622, (617) 863-1876
Price: $295 (*EyeRelief*), $49.95 (*No-Squint Cursor Enhancer*)

Filch
Kinetic Designs Inc.
14231 Anatevka Lane, SE
Olalla, WA 98466
(800) 453-0330, (206) 857-7943
Price: $130

FreeBoard
Pointer Systems, Inc.
One Mill St.
Burlington, VT 05401
(800) 537-1562, (802) 658-3260
Price: $695 ($1395 with *FreeWheel*)
Requires: Any mouse emulator
(MS-DOS)
In Short: Half screen keyboard
emulator that works with any mouse
emulating device, but is particularly
appropriate for those devices that
readily result in larger movements,
such as electronic head pointers. On
screen keyboard includes lexical
prediction and is highly customizable. When used with *FreeWheel*, letter (or word) selection is done via
time delay, thus negating the need
for a switch (or mouse button depression). Many parameters are
easily adjusted, and entire virtual
keyboards can be designed from
scratch (although such work is very
complex). *FreeBoard* requires the undivided attention of the mouse
driver, and is therefore not compatible with graphically based applications.

FreeWheel
Pointer Systems, Inc.
One Mill St.
Burlington, VT 05401
(800) 537-1562, (802) 658-3260
Price: $1195 ($1395 with *FreeBoard*)
Requires: Serial (MS-DOS) or ADB
(Mac) port
In Short: An optical pointing device that provides mouse emulation,

using infrared light. A light-weight reflector is worn on any point control sight, but is usually worn on the forehead. The reflector emulates directional mouse movement only, a separate switch must be used to click the mouse buttons. While offering maximum convenience (user not way tethered to the computer) device is often impractical for graphically based applications because there is too much difficulty in controlling the mouse pointer. Proper position of the reflector and user in front of the optical camera is crucial. *FreeWheel* works well with its companion product, *FreeBoard,* a keyboard emulator.

HeadMaster

Prentke Romich Company
1022 Heyl Rd.
Wooster, OH 44691
(800) 642-8255, (216) 262-1984
  Price: $1095
  Requires: Serial (MS-DOS) or ADB (Mac) port
  In Short: Electronic (ultrasonic) head pointing device that provides mouse emulation. Control is excellent, and user can "recenter" mouse pointer as needed. The headset tethers the user to the computer due to the necessary cable. Single button mouse clicking is achieved by switch activation, usually via the provided sip-and-puff switch. Since the sip-and-puff switch moves with the headset fine (or gross) movement (with or without mouse button activation) is easy with the Prentke Romich adapters that allow the *HeadMaster* to work with IBM compatible computers and ADB Macintoshes, and features of the original Macintosh version are lost.
  If you want the MS-DOS version

of the *HeadMaster,* try AbiliTech (see entry for "*AbiliCAD*"). For the same $1095 price, AbiliTech adds enhancements such as an additional button access. AbiliTech also offers an adaptor that is based on a Logitech bus mouse and the ability to easily switch between the mouse and *HeadMaster.*

Ke:nx

Don Johnston Development Equipment, Inc.
P.O. Box 639
1000 N. Rand Rd., Bldg. 15
Wauconda, IL 60084-0639
(800) 999-4660, (708) 526-2682
  Price: $780
  Requires: ADB port (Macintosh only)
  In Short: A flexible system for providing multiple access to the Apple Macintosh line of computers. Access modalities include assisted keyboard, one or multiple switches (both morse code and scanning), and alternative keyboards. Mouse emulation is not proportional, but it is highly programmable, as are the various keyboard layouts. The interface box (for attaching switches and alternative keyboards) also provides hardware copy protection.

Kurzweil Voicesystem (discontinued)

Kurzweil Applied Intelligence Inc.
411 Waverly Oaks Rd.
Waltham, MA 02154
(617) 893-5151
  Price: $6500

Liaison

Du-It Control Systems Group
8765 Township Rd. #513
Shreve, OH 44676
(216) 567-2906
  Price: $3930

Requires: Any PC or Apple ADB computer

In Short: A microcomputer in and of itself, the *Liaison* is controlled via a proportional chin (or tongue) joystick, and could be the same device used to control a Du-It brand wheelchair. *Liaison* provides complete and transparent keyboard and mouse emulation, as well as the ability to turn the computer (and peripherals) on and off independently. The keyboard emulation functions include macro abilities and abbreviations/expansion. Environmental controls, including complete phone access and X-10 compatibility, are also included. All functions are customizable.

MagicWand Keyboard
In-Touch Systems
Eleven Westview Rd.
Spring Valley, NY 10977
(914) 354-7431
Price: $1295
Requires: Standard PC mouse connector
In Short: An adaptive replacement keyboard designed for small movement, lite strength requirements, or mouth-stick users. Keyboard emulation is hardware based and transparent to applications. Keyboard includes macro generating abilities. A mouse emulator add-on (see *McKey Mouse*) is also available.

McKey Mouse
In-Touch Systems
Eleven Westview Rd.
Spring Valley, NY 10977
(914) 354-7431
Price: $295
Requires: MagicWand Keyboard, serial port
In Short: An adaptive mouse emulator that uses the *MagicWand Key-* board as the pointing area. Mouse pointing is not proportional, but can be readily sped up or slowed down. All keyboard functions remain accessible.

Microsoft Mouse, MS-DOS 5.0 (MicroSoft Disk Operating System), Microsoft Excel 3.0, Microsoft Windows 3.0, Microsoft Works 2.0
Microsoft Corporation
One Microsoft Way
Redmond, WA 98052-6399
(800) 426-9400, (206) 697-1317
Price: $125 *(mouse),* $100 *(MS-DOS),* $495 *(Excel),* $150 *(Windows),* $295 *(Works)*
Requires: Serial port or bus (MS-DOS only)
In Short: Mice are especially good for free-hand drawing and paint applications, as they are very "natural" to use once you have had some training. Mice use the whole arm and several fingers to operate, which affords good control but makes them unwieldy for many people with even modest movement impairments. In use, a mouse must have its orientation maintained, and often requires being lifted and moved over the desktop surface. Their accuracy is usually limited to 200 dots per inch (dpi), although 300 dpi models are available. Mice vary in the ergonomics of their design, the number of buttons (usually two or three), how they interface with the computer. Cordless (radio or infrared controlled) mice are available. Most major brands of mice include utilities for adjusting the display/control ratio of the mouse driver and for creating menus for programs that don't normally support a mouse.

Many, many other brands of mice are available. Other brands usually are *Microsoft Mouse* compatible.

MindReader, Version 2.0
Brown Bag Software
2155 S. Bascom Ave., Suite 114
Campbell, CA 95008
(800) 523-0764, (800) 823-5335
Price: $90

OmniKey/ULTRA
Northgate Computer Systems, Inc.
7075 Flying Cloud Dr.
Eden Prairie, MN 55344
(800) 526-2446, (612) 943-8181
Price: $99
Requires: Standard PC mouse connector
In Short: A most flexible replacement keyboard. Includes such desirable features as click/tactile mechanical key switches, some switchable keys, duel (latching) function keys, optional Dvorak layout, repeat/delay rate settings, and keyboard serialization features. Less expensive ($89) versions (the *OmniKey/101* and *102*) that do away with the extra set of function keys, but retain all the other features, are available. Many other brands of replacement keyboards are available.

PC-TRAC/MacTRAC
MicroSpeed Incorporated
44000 Old Warm Spring Blvd.
Fremont, CA 94538
(415) 490-1403
Price: $119
Requires: Serial (MS-DOS) or ADB (Mac) port
In Short: An excellent trackball. A PC bus version is also available ($139). Track balls have the advantage over mice in that they are stationary and require less desk space.

In terms of adaptive access, they are often quite useable by persons with a broad range of disability, especially with appropriate positioning. Like mice, trackball vary widely in quality. Things to look for in a trackball: (1) ergonomic design, (2) the ability to buttons while moving the trackball, (3) the ability to adjust the display/control ratio of the trackball rotation to mouse pointer movement. Many other brands of trackballs are available.

Pearl Corder
Sharper Image
650 Davis St.
San Francisco, CA
(415) 445-6000
Price: $199

PRD+, Version 2.0
Productivity Software International
211 E. 43rd St. #2202
New York, NY 10017-4707
(800) 533-7587, (212) 967-8666
Price: $280–$430 (depending on features)

ProKey Plus, Version 5.0
RoseSoft Inc.
P.O. Box 79337
Bellevue, WA 98007
(206) 562-0225
Price: $100

QuattroPro 4.0, SideKick for the Macintosh 2.0, SideKick 2, Super-Key 2.0, Turbo Lightning
Borland International, Inc.
1800 Green Hills Rd.
P.O. Box 66001
455 Scotts Valley, CA 95006-0001
(800) 331-0877
Retail Prices: $495 *(QuattroPro),* $100 *(SideKick/Mac, SuperKey, Turbo Lightning),* $200 *(SideKick 2)*

Spelling Coach Professional 3.01
Deneba Software
3305 N.W. 74th Ave.
Miami, FL 33122
(305) 594-6965, (800) 622-6827
  Price: $199

SummaSketch II
Summagraphics Corporation
Sixty Silvermine Rd.
Seymour, CT 06483-3907
(800) 243-9388, (203) 881-5400
  Price: $599
  Requires: Serial (MS-DOS) or ADB
(Mac) port
  In Short: Graphics tablets. Tablets
are especially good for fast and accurate digitizing, tracing, drawing,
cursor steering, and menu picking
with CAD or graphics software.
Tablets (in general) are extremely
precise, the *SummaSketch* series have
a resolution of over a thousand lines
per inch. The tablets typically provides both a screen pointing area
and menu (macro) choice section.
The *SummaSketch* series include
specific drivers for AutoDesk products and *Microsoft Windows,* as well
as a utility for emulating a *Microsoft
Mouse.* Many other brands of digitizing tablets are available. Other
brands are usually Summagraphics
compatible.

Super3D 3.1, SuperPaint 2.0
Silicon Beach Software
P.O. Box 261430
San Diego, CA 92126
(619) 695-6956
  Prices: $495 *(Super3D),* $199 *(Super-
Paint 2.0)*

**Symantec Utilities for the Macintosh
  (SUM II)**
Symantec
10201 Torre Ave.
Cupertino, CA 85014
(408) 253-9600
  Price: $150

WordWriter
McIntyre Computer Systems
22809 Shagbark
Birmingham, MI 48010
(313) 645-5090
  Price: $100

Appendix B:
Selected Glossary

8088, 8086, 80286, 80386, 80486 are the names of chips introduced by Intel. These numbers also refer to computers built around these chips. As we go up in the series chips become more powerful and faster, and the machines become more expensive. It is pretty well the case that any program that will run on a machine at the beginning of the series will run on a machine higher up, but the converse is not necessarily true. Typically these machines are MS-DOS, although they can run other operating systems. The 80386 and 80486 have several advantages besides power over the 80286 (and other previous CPU chips) in terms of multi-tasking and memory management. Any IBM compatible machine that is sophisticated enough to effectively employ a graphical user interface (GUI) is going to be based on the 80386 or 80486, or the less powerful versions, the 80386sx and the 80486sx. The 80386 is roughly equivalent in processing power to Motorola's 68030, which is used in the advanced Apple Macintosh computers.

8514A One of the first Super VGA displays pioneered by IBM. 8514A (actually the model number) specifies an interlaced display of up to 1024 by 768 pixels, using 16 colors. Like all other Super VGA standards, application support for it is uncommon.

AT Model of second generation computers introduced by IBM. The AT was the first 16 bit PC and is based on Intel's 80286 microprocessor. It continues to have a huge installed base. "AT compatible" is often advertised by clone makers. The AT introduced new features, many of which (such as the 16 bit bus and the "101" enhanced keyboard) have become standards. The 80286 is roughly equivalent in processing power to Motorola's 68020, which was used in the original Apple Macintosh II.

CAD, CADD Computer Aided Design, Computer Aided Design and Drafting.

CGA Color Graphics Adaptor. The first color monitor standards established by IBM. It specifies a screen resolution of 320 by 200 pixels using four colors. This resolution is not sufficient for usable graphics.

clone   A computer that is fully compatible with some other manufacturer's brand of computer. Usually refers to IBM compatibility. The "open architecture" of the first IBM PC's enabled clones to be legally available.

CPU   Central Processing Unit. The microprocessor which is the main "brain" of a microcomputer.

EISA   Enhanced Industry Standard Architecture. Pronounced "e'-sa." A public domain standard for extending the ISA bus standards from 16 to 32 bits. An EISA bus has the desirable feature that it will accept both 8 and 16 bit ISA cards as well as 32 bit EISA cards.

Expanded and **Extended Memory**   An artifact of the original XT computer and MS-DOS is that memory access is severely limited. Extended memory refers to any memory above 640K, while Expanded memory is memory above 640K that follows certain standards (LIM 4.0 EMS).

FPU   Floating Point Unit. ALU (Arithmetic Logic Unit) is also used. Mathematics coprocessor. Used to off-load floating point calculations from the CPU. Dramatically improves the speed of some applications, such as CAD and spreadsheets. FPU are an upgrade option for almost all computers. Intel 80486 based computers.

GUI   Graphical User Interface. Pronounced "gooey." The way a person (the "user") works and interacts with a program (the "interface") is graphically (as opposed to text) based. Such applications almost always involve some sort of pointing device (usually a mouse), icons, and more sophisticated computers. There are *many* different GUI environments.

IBM   International Business Machines. IBM introduced a PC in the early 1980s that continues to define the lowest common denominator in business and home use computers. IBM compatible is synonymous with MS-DOS compatible.

icon   A small stylized picture representing some computer activity, such as starting ("launching") an application or executing a command that is typically activated by a mouse or similar pointing device. Icons can represent files, disks, printers, etcetera.

Interlaced   A technique whereby the display on a monitor is generated in two passes (every other line). Usually seen only with higher resolution (Super VGA) displays. Interlaced monitors are much less expensive than non-interlaced.

IRQ   Interrupt ReQuest. An integral feature of ISA that controls communication along the bus. No two bus cards are allowed to have the same IRQ number. Alleviating such conflicts (by setting jumpers and dip switches) is also tedious and time consuming.

ISA Industry Standard Architecture. Refers primarily to the 16 bit bus of IBM's original "AT" computer. May also refer to the 8 bit bus employed by IBM's original "XT" model computer.

Mac, Macintosh A line of computers introduced by Apple (makers of the Apple II) in the early 1980s. Mac's (as they are familiarly known) were the first computer to popularize a graphical user interface. The first Macintoshes (and the *Mac Classic*) used the Motorola 68000 for their CPU. Faster Macs (the Macintosh II's) use Motorola's 68020 and the 68030.

MCA Micro Channel Architecture. A 32 bit bus standard employed by IBM (and some others) in their PS/2 line of microcomputers. MCA (and NuBus) has the advantage over ISA in that peripherals can be self-configuring. User settings of dip switches and jumpers is not necessary.

mouse A pointing device operated by one hand that moves a mouse cursor (pointer, arrow, cross-hairs) on a computer screen. Use of a mouse typically involves pressing ("clicking") one or more buttons (simultaneously) when the mouse cursor is at a desired position, double clicking (two or more presses in quick secession), and moving the mouse cursor while holding down one or more buttons ("dragging"). Not all applications require all these movements. Many different pointing devices can substitute for a mouse.

MS-DOS MicroSoft Disk Operating System. Base operating system for IBM computers and compatibles. Also simply referred to as DOS. A computer that can completely run MS-DOS is an IBM compatible or "clone."

multitasking The ability of the computer (or operating system) to allow work on several different applications simultaneously. A user has the ability to quickly and smoothly shift tasks and even whole applications.

NuBus The 16 to 32 bit buses used in Macintosh II computers. There are several different NuBus standards.

OS/2 A sophisticated multitasking GUI operating system developed by IBM.

PC Personal Computer. Also the model name used by IBM in one of their early computers (PC-XT).

Pixel From "picture element." The smallest addressable unit of a computer screen (less commonly, printer or scanner). The resolution of monitors is measured in pixels (horizontal by vertical), with more being better.

RAM Random Access Memory. The computers "thinking space." Measures how much (as opposed to how well) a computer can work on at a time. One megabyte (1024K) of RAM is common. Computers designed for today's GUI's will have at least two megabytes or RAM with four, eight, or sixteen megabytes not being uncommon.

SCSI   Small Computer System Interface. Pronounced "scuzzy." A high level interface protocol used with some systems for communication between a computer and data intensive peripherals (such as hard drives, CD-ROM drives, scanners, and printers). A SCSI port is a feature of Macintosh computers.

Super VGA   Not actually a graphics standard, but refers to a display system (IBM Compatible) that is a super-set of the VGA graphic standards (see below). Common resolutions (in pixels) are: 640 by 480 (with 256, or more, colors simultaneously), 800 by 600, 1024 by 768, and 1280 by 1024. Even higher resolutions are possible.

System 7   The latest operating system for the Apple Macintosh line of computers. It is a sophisticated, multitasking GUI.

VGA   Video Gate Array. The last graphics standard to be established (and completely accepted) in the IBM compatible world. It specifies a screen resolution of 640 by 480 pixels, using up to 16 colors simultaneously (out of a palette of over 16.7 million colors), or 640 by 200 pixels, using 256 colors.

Windows 3.0   A multitasking GUI for MS-DOS based compatibles threatens to replace MS-DOS as the common operating environment for a majority of computers. Windows makes severe demand upon PC's, to the extent that XT and AT computers effectively cannot run it.

XGA   The latest graphics offering from IBM specifies a noninterlaced display of up to 1280 by 1024 pixels, using 256 colors. It is one of many Super VGA standards and does not have wide support from applications.

XT   Refers to a model of computer, popularized by IBM early in the 1980s. XT compatibility refers to a broad range of computers, but refers to those based on Intel's 8088, and 8086, microprocessor, and NEC's V20 microprocessor. XT computers employ an eight bit architecture. The 8086 is roughly equivalent in processing power to Motorola's 68000 (although that is a 16 bit chip).

Appendix C:
State Resources

Under the so called Harkin Act the National Institute on Disability and Rehabilitation Research competitively funds state technology centers. As of 1991 the centers that follow were funded. These institutions are good stops for information in your state.

Alaska

Ms. Joyce Palmer
Program Coordinator
Alaska Assistive Technology Services
Division of Vocational Rehabilitation
400 D St., Suite 230
Anchorage, AK 99501
(907) 274-0138
FAX: (907) 274-0516
Assistive Technology Project

Arkansas

Ms. Sue Gaskin
Project Director
Department of Human Services
Division of Rehabilitation Services
Increasing Capabilities Access Network
2201 Brookwood Dr., Suite 117
Little Rock, AR 72202

(501) 666-8868, (800) 828-2799 (In-State)
FAX: (501) 666-5319

Colorado

Mr. Donald St. Louis
Executive Director
Rocky Mountain Resource and Training Institute (RMRTI)
6355 Ward Road—Suite 310
Arvada, CO 80004
(303) 420-2942
FAX: (303) 420-8675

Delaware

Beth A. Mineo, Ph.D.
University of Delaware
Center for Applied Science and Engineering
New Castle County
Newark, DE 19716
(302) 651-6830

Georgia

Ms. Joy Kniskern
Georgia Department of Human Resources
Georgia Division of Rehabilitation Services

878 Peachtree St., NE
Rm. 702
Atlanta, GA 30309
(404) 853-9151

Hawaii

Mr. Neil Shim
Department of Human Services
Vocational Rehabilitation and Ser-
    vices for the Blind Division
1000 Bishop St., Rm. 605
Honolulu, HI 96813
(808) 586-5368

Illinois

Ms. Pennie Cooper
Executive Director
Illinois Assistive Technology Project
Department of Rehabilitation Ser-
    vices
Division of Planning and Special
    Initiatives
411 East Adams St.
Springfield, IL 62701
(217) 522-7985
FAX: (217) 522-8067

Indiana

Ms. Sandra Metcalf
Project Manager
Indiana Department of Human Ser-
    vices
Office of Vocational Rehabilitation
Technology Assistance Unit
150 W. Market St.
P.O. Box 7083
Indianapolis, IN 46207-7083
(317) 233-3394
Technology-Related Assistance for
    Individuals with Disabilities

Iowa

James C. Hardy, Ph.D.
Director
Iowa Program for Assistive Technol-
    ogy
University Hospital School
Iowa City, IA 52242
(319) 353-6386
FAX: (319) 356-8284
Technology-Related Assistance for
    Individuals with Disabilities

Kentucky

Ms. Janice Weber
Director
Kentucky Assistive Technology Ser-
    vice (KATS) Network
427 Versailles Rd.
Frankfort, KY 40601
(502) 564-4665, (800) 327-KATS
FAX: (502) 564-3976

Louisiana

Anne E. Farber, Ph.D.
Louisiana State Planning Council
    on Developmental Disabilities
Department of Health and Hospitals
P.O. Box 3455
Baton Rouge, LA 70821-3455
(504) 342-6804

Maine

Mr. David Noble Stockford
Director
Division of Special Education
Maine Department of Education
State House Station #23
Augusta, ME 04330
(207) 289-5950, (207) 289-2550 (TDD)
FAX: (207) 289-5900

Maryland

Mr. Jay Brill
Director
Maryland Technology Assistance
  Project
Governor's Office for Handicapped
  Individuals
300 W. Lexington St.
1 Market Center — Box 10
Baltimore, MD 21201
(301) 333-3098
FAX: (301) 555-3280

Massachusetts

Ms. Nancy V. Robbins
Deputy Commissioner for Policy
  and Programs
Commission for the Deaf & Hard of
  Hearing
Central Office
600 Washington St., Rm. 600
Boston, MA 02111
(617) 727-5106
Massachusetts Assistive Technology
  Partnership (MATP)

Minnesota

Ms. Rachel Wobschall
Executive Director
Star Program
Minnesota State Planning Agency
300 Centennial Bldg.
658 Cedar St.
St. Paul, MN 55155
(612) 297-1554
FAX: (612) 296-3698

Mississippi

Mr. H. P. (Pete) Martin
Director

Division of Rehabilitation Services
Department of Human Services
300 Capers Ave.
Jackson, MS 39203
(601) 354-6891
Project START — Success Through
  Assistive/Rehabilitative Technol-
  ogy

Missouri

Carl F. Calkins, Ph.D.
Curators of the State of Missouri
UMKC Institute for Human Devel-
  opment
Office of Research Administration
University of Missouri — Kansas City
Kansas City, MO 64110
(816) 276-1755

Montana

Mr. William D. Lamb
Montana Department of Social and
  Rehabilitation Services
Rehabilitative Services Division
111 Sanders
P.O. Box 4210
Helena, MT 59604
(406) 444-2590

Nebraska

Mr. Mark Schultz
Project Director
Assistive Technology Project
Nebraska Department of Education
Division of Rehabilitation Services
301 Centennial Mall South
P.O. Box 94987
Lincoln, NE 68509-4987
(402) 471-0735, (800) 742-7594
FAX: (402) 471-2701

Nevada

Ms. Donny Loux
Chief
Program Development
Rehabilitation Division, PRPD
505 E. King St., Rm. 502
Carson City, NV 89710
(702) 885-4440
Assistive Technology Services, Ad-
    vocacy, and Systems Change

New Hampshire

Ms. Jan Nisbet
Commissioner of Education
New Hampshire State Department
    of Education
Department of Education
State of New Hampshire
Concord, NH 03824
(603) 362-4320

New Mexico

Mr. Andy Winnegar
Director
New Mexico TAP
State Department of Education
Division of Vocational Rehabilitation
604 W. San Mateo
Santa Fe, NM 87505
(505) 827-3520
New Mexico Technology Related
    Assistance Program (NMTAP)

New York

Ms. Deborah V. Buck
Project Manager
NY State Office of Advocate for the
    Disabled
TRAID Project
One ESP—10th Floor

Albany, NY 12223-0001
(518) 473-4129
Technology-Related Assistance of
    Individuals with Disabilities
    (TRAID)

North Carolina

Ms. Ricki Cook
Project Director
North Carolina Assistive Technol-
    ogy Project
Department of Human Resources
Division of Vocational Rehabilita-
    tion Services
1110 Navaho Dr., Suite 101
Raleigh, NC 27609
(919) 850-2787
North Carolina Assistive Technol-
    ogy Project

Oregon

Gregory Fishwick, Ph.D., N.C.C.
TALN Project Director
Oregon Vocational Rehabilitation
    Division
Department of Human Resources
2045 Silverton Rd., NE
Salem, OR 97310
(503) 378-3850 (Voice/TDD)
Technology Access for Life Needs
    (TALN)

South Carolina

Mr. Joe S. Dusenbury
South Carolina Vocational Rehabili-
    tation Department
P.O. Box 15
West Columbia, SC 29171-0015
(803) 822-5303
Contact Person: P. Charles LaRosa
    (803) 822-5303

Tennessee

Mr. E. H. (Buddy) Wright
Project Director
Tennessee Technology Access Project
Department of Mental Health and Mental Retardation
3rd Fl., Doctors' Bldg.
706 Church St.
Nashville, TN 37243-0675
(615) 741-3807
Tennessee Technology Access Project (TTAP)

Utah

Dr. Marvin Fifield
Director
Utah Assistive Technology Program (UATP)
Utah State University
Developmental Center for Handicapped Persons
Logan, UT 84322-6855
(801) 750-1982
FAX: (801) 750-2044

Vermont

Mr. Jesse Barth
Director
Assistive Technology Project
Department of Aging and Disabilities
Agency of Human Services
103 S. Main St.

Waterbury, VT 05676
(802) 241-2186
FAX: (802) 244-8103
Assistive Technology Development Grant

Virginia

Mr. Kenneth H. Knorr, Jr.
Director
Virginia Assistive Technology System
Department of Rehabilitative Services
4901 Fitzhugh Ave.
P.O. Box 11045
Richmond, VA 23230
(804) 367-0316 (TDD)
(804) 367-0315 (TDD)
(800) 552-5019
FAX: (804) 367-9256
Developing a Model System for Accessing Assistive Technology

Wisconsin

Ms. Judi Trampf
Acting Director
WisTech
Division of Vocational Rehabilitation
1 W. Wilson St., Rm. 950
P.O. Box 7852
Madison, WI 53702
(608) 266-1281 (Voice)
(608) 266-9599 (TDD)
State Grants Program, Technology-Related Assistance for Individuals with Disabilities

Appendix D:
Organizations

The following five organizations may be useful starting points. In any event, you should consult the extensive list of organizations, not all about computing, which follow them.

Alliance for Technology Access
(formerly The National Special Education Alliance)
National Offices: ask for the address of the ATA Center in your state
1307 Solano Ave.
Albany, CA 94706-1888
(510) 528-0747

217 Massachusetts Ave.
Lexington, MA 02173
(617) 863-9966

Apple Computer
(800) 732-3131 × 950
24 hours/day
Disability Solution Group: (408) 974-7910
   Information on local dealers, users groups. Request videotapes(); brochure (Toward Independence). Using computers in special education, and more.

IBM Special Needs Information and Referral Center
(800) 426-2133
8:30AM–5:15PM EST
   Information on local dealers, user groups. Application forms for loans, grants and discounts. Awareness information. Printed resource guides related to different disability groups, including information on products. Request videotapes (5) on IBM independence series products.

American Foundation for the Blind (AFB)
National Technology Center
15 West 16th St.
New York, NY 10011
(212) 620-2000

Trace Center, Information Service
1500 Highland Ave.
University of Wisconsin
Madison, WI 53705
(608) 262-6966

ABLEDATA
Newington Children's Hospital
Adaptive Equipment Center
181 E. Cedar St.
Newington, CT 06111
(203) 667-5405, (800) 344-5405
   ABLEDATA is a computerized listing of over 17,000 commercially available products for rehabilitation and independent living. Annotations about each product give detailed descriptions. Computer owners may obtain an individual copy of ABLEDATA

through the Trace Center (below). Professionals or others who subscribe to Bibliographic Retrieval Services (BRS) may access ABLEDATA directly. For information about BRS, (800) 289-4277.

ABLENET
1081 10th Ave. S.E.
Minneapolis, MN 55414
(612) 379-0956
ABLENET provides information on technological devices and support services for children and adults with severe or profound disabilities.

Access Specialists, Inc.
4366 Edgewood Ave.
Oakland, CA 94602
(415) 548-5752
Access Specialists, Inc. (ASI) is a consulting firm specializing in disability-related laws and regulations.

ACT Test Administration
P.O. Box 168
Iowa City, IA 52243
(319) 337-1332
ACT (American College Testing) can respond to some needs for special arrangements at its regular testing centers, although large-type or braille editions or audiocassette tapes are not available there. With proper documentation of the disability, individual administrations of the assessment can be arranged for those students with physical or perceptual disabilities who cannot attend established test centers, take the tests within the allotted time using regular-type test booklets, or who are confined to hospitals on all scheduled test dates. Call or write for a Request for Special Testing.

Adaptive Living
Adaptive Living Rehabilitation
  Engineering Services
30 Northampton St.
Rochester, NY 14606
(716) 458-5455
Adaptive Living is a rehabilitation engineering service. The company recommends, designs, and modifies equipment and devices to allow people with disabilities to lead as productive a life as possible at home or on the job.

AIDS Action Council
2033 M St., NW, Suite 802
Washington, DC 20036
(202) 293-2886
The Council is an advocacy group which monitors legislation and public policy affecting people with AIDS. It provides a voice for community-based service organizations rather than direct service referral for individuals. A legislative newsletter is available.

Alexander Graham Bell Association for the Deaf
3417 Volta Place NW
Washington, DC 20007
(202) 337-5220
This national organization offers support services to deaf individuals and teachers, speech-language pathologists, audiologists, physicians, and parents of hearing impaired students. It promotes speech, lipreading, and use of residual hearing by hearing impaired individuals.

Alliance for Technology Access
Foundation for Technology Access
1307 Solano Ave.
Albany, CA 94706-188
(415) 528-0747
The Alliance for Technology

Access (ATA; formerly the National Special Education Alliance) is a coalition of over forty resource centers. Each center in the ATA operates autonomously under a separate name and has its own area of expertise. The ATA centers all share a grass-roots orientation: the belief that meaningful and lasting change starts at the local level. At every center, people try out equipment and compare experiences. The centers host workshops, lectures, product demonstrations and open houses. All ATA centers are electronically linked to each other as well as to major national databases and bulletin boards. Individual ATA centers receive financial and technical support from various local industries and third-party vendors, as well as from civic organizations and local foundations.

American Academy for Cerebral Palsy and Developmental Medicine
2315 Westwood Ave.
Richmond, VA 23230
(804) 355-0147
This professional organization concentrates on the latest developments in the treatment of cerebral palsy. It is concerned with diagnosis, care, treatment, and research into cerebral palsy and developmental disorders. Members include occupational therapists, physical therapists, and speech-language pathologists.

American Alliance for Health, Phys. Ed., Recreation and Dance
1900 Association Dr.
Reston, VA 22091
(703) 476-3400
The Alliance is a membership organization of professionals in the fields of physical education, recreation, health and safety, and dance. Their Adapted Physical Activity Council has a nationwide network to provide information about adapting curricula and activities to the needs of people with disabilities. Back copies of the journal, *Able Bodies,* and other publications are available.

American Amputee Foundation
2506 Riverfront Dr. #3
Little Rock, AR 72202
(501) 666-2523
The Amputee Foundation services amputees and their families, offers peer support, direct aid, hospital visitation, self-help, and general publications.

American Association for Counseling and Development (AACD)
5999 Stevenson Ave.
Alexandria, VA 22304
(703) 823-9800, (703) 370-1943 (TDD)
AACD is the parent organization for counselors from educational and social service settings across the country who have joined one or more of 15 subdivisions of AACD. Included are postsecondary, secondary, and elementary school counselors; vocational counselors; mental health, employment, and diagnostic/ evaluation rehabilitation counselors; and other interested professionals. Each group has its own newsletter, publications, and conferences. AACD can furnish a publications list.

American Association for the Advancement of Science (AAAS)
Project on Science, Technology, and Disability

1333 H St., N.W.
Washington, DC 20005
(202) 326-6667 (Voice/TDD)

The Project addresses the concerns of scientists and engineers with disabilities, and offers suggestions about improving accessibility of science programs for students with disabilities. *The Directory of Scientists and Engineers with Disabilities* (2nd Edition, 1987) lists people in various parts of the country who are available for consultation ($10, plus $3 postage). *Science for Handicapped Students in Higher Education* is out of print but available in many college libraries. *Scientific and Engineering Societies: Resources for Career Planning,* edited by Martha Redden and Virginia Stern, offers counselors and students an overview of the wide range of career possibilities and level of education required in science and engineering ($6, prepaid to AAAS Sales Dept.) *Access to the Science and Engineering Laboratory and Classroom* (1986) is available free from AAAS or from HEATH. Available free is a 1991 series entitled *Barrier-Free in Brief,* covering four topics: workshops and conferences for scientists and engineers, classrooms and laboratories in science and engineering, access in word and deed, and access to science literacy.

American Association of Collegiate Registrars and Admissions Officers (AACRAO)
One Dupont Circle, Suite 330
Washington, DC 20036
(202) 293-9161

AACRAO is a non-profit, voluntary, professional, education association of degree-granting postsecondary institutions, government agencies, private educational organiza-

tions, and education-oriented businesses in the United States and abroad. Its goal is to promote higher education and further the professional development of members working in admissions, enrollment management, financial aid, institutional research, records and registration. AACRAO and HEATH have jointly published *Recruitment, Admissions, and Handicapped Students.* This guide provides practical suggestions for implementation of the law. It is available free from either organization.

American Association of Disability Communicators (AADC)
c/o National Easter Seal Society
70 E. Lake St.
Chicago, IL 60601
(312) 726-6200, (312) 726-4258 (TDD)

AADC is an information network among communicators (such as writers, reporters, and television/radio news broadcasters) who address issues relevant to people with disabilities. Examples of these issues are media coverage, media access, transportation access, and the language used to describe people with disabilities.

American Association of the Deaf-Blind (AADB)
814 Thayer Ave.
Silver Spring, MD 20910
(301) 588-6545

AADB is a national consumer advocacy organization for people who have combined hearing and vision impairments. It holds an annual convention and has chapters around the country. It provides technical assistance to deaf-blind persons, families, educators, and service providers. Annual dues are $12.

American Association on Mental Retardation (AAMR)
1719 Kalorama Rd., NW
Washington, DC 20009
(202) 387-1719, (800) 424-3688

AAMR is an interdisciplinary association of professionals and concerned individuals in the field of mental retardation. National and regional meetings, as well as publications, serve to inform members about the latest research and practices. Publications include the *American Journal on Mental Retardation;* a bimonthly journal called *Mental Retardation;* and *News & Notes,* a quarterly newsletter. Regional units have additional services, including some scholarship aid for students.

American Chemical Society
1155 Sixteenth St., NW
Washington, DC 20036
(202) 872-4438

The Society's Committee on the Handicapped publishes a manual entitled *Teaching Chemistry to Physically Handicapped Students.*

American Council of the Blind (ACB)
1155 15th St., NW, Suite 720
Washington, DC 20005
(202) 467-5081, (800) 424-8666

ACB is an information referral and advocacy agency. There are 52 state/regional affiliates and 21 national special interest and professional affiliates. Their goal is to improve the well-being of people who are blind or visually impaired through legislative advocacy; to improve educational and rehabilitation facilities, encourage and assist all blind persons to develop their abilities; and conduct a public education program to promote greater understanding of blind people.

American Council on Rural Special Education (ACRES)
National Rural Development Institute
Miller Hall 359
Western Washington University
Bellingham, WA 98225
(206) 676-3576

Dedicated to the interests of individuals with disabilities living in rural areas, ACRES publishes the *ACRES Ruralink,* a quarterly newsletter. Also available is a 1987 publication, *Rural Transition Strategies That Work* ($5). The $45 membership fee provides access to a job referral service, conferences, monographs, and other resources.

American Deafness and Rehabilitation Association
P.O. Box 55369
Little Rock, AR 72225
(501) 375-6643

The American Deafness and Rehabilitation Association is an organization of rehabilitation counselors, clergy, social workers, physicians, psychologists, audiologists, speech therapists and other professionals in allied fields whose major concern is the provision of professional services to deaf adults. Biannual national conferences are held. The organization sponsors workshops, conferences and publications on all aspects of deafness.

American Foundation for the Blind, Inc.
15 W. 16th St.
New York, NY 10011
(800) 232-5463, (212) 620-2080

American Foundation for the Blind is a national organization and a network of local resources for blind and visually impaired persons. It offers a variety of services: education, employment, orientation and mobility, and rehabilitation.

American Institute of Architects (AIA)
c/o Information Center
1735 New York Ave., NW
Washington, DC 20006
(202) 626-7493

The Institute has published two annotated bibliographies of material on barrier-free design. One bibliography lists 60 books, and the other offers 13 pages of references to periodical articles. Both are free to AIA members ($10 each for non-members) upon request.

American Occupational Therapy Association
1383 Piccard Dr.
Rockville, MD 20850
(301) 948-9626

American Occupational Therapy Association is a nationwide organization of professionals concerned with all aspects of the occupational therapy field. The organization publishes the *American Journal of Occupational Therapy.*

American Printing House for the Blind, Inc. (APH)
1839 Frankfort Ave.
P.O. Box 6085
Louisville, KY 40206-0085
(502) 895-2405

APH, established in 1858, manufactures materials for the use of blind people of all ages. Reading materials include books in braille, large type, and recorded form. Edu-

cational aids, tools, and supplies include braille writing and embossing equipment; computer software and hardware; educational games; low vision aids; braille and large type paper, binders, and notebooks. It will ship products to any destination in the world, and the catalogues are available in print and on cassette.

American Self-Help Clearinghouse
St. Clares-Riverside Medical Center
Pocono Rd.
Denville, NJ 07834
(201) 625-7101, (201) 625-9053 (TDD)

The Clearinghouse provides information on a wide range of self-help groups and state/local self-help clearinghouses. It publishes a directory of national and model groups, *The Self-Help Sourcebook.* Staff can provide consultation on starting new types of self-help networks or groups.

American Society of Allied Health Professions (ASAHP)
1101 Connecticut Ave., NW, Suite 700
Washington, DC 20036-4387
(202) 857-1150

ASAHP publishes *Trends,* a monthly newsletter for allied health professionals which includes information about integrating people with disabilities into the field. It also publishes *Alliances in Health and Education: Serving Youngsters with Special Needs,* which includes an instructors' guide of strategies for teaching and ways to incorporate relevant topics into curricula, workshops, and conferences ($19.95). Their *Journal* ($65) and *Trends* ($40) are included with membership. Contact ASAHP for details.

**American Speech-Language-
Hearing Association (ASHA)**
10801 Rockville Pike
Rockville, MD 20852
(301) 897-5700

American Speech-Language-
Hearing Association (ASHA) is the
largest professional organization for
speech-language pathologists and
audiologists. The organization is involved in a number of different applications of computer technology in
the areas of speech and language,
including administration, clinic,
therapy, school, and research.

**American Speech-Language-
Hearing Foundation**
10801 Rockville Pike
Rockville, MD 20852
(301) 897-5700

The American Speech-Language-
Haaring Foundation (ASHF) works
to advance knowledge and improve
practice in serving children and
adults who have speech, language or
hearing disorders. Through the support of its contributors, the Foundation allocates funds for scholarships,
for research and for special projects.

APH-CARL
American Printing House for the
Blind
P.O. Box 6085
Louisville, KY 40206-0085
(502) 895-2405

The American Printing House for
the Blind's CARL (Central Automated Resource List) provides professionals and volunteers in the field
of blindness with immediate access
to a range of information about materials for educating students who
are visually impaired or blind.

Apple Computer, Inc.
**National Special Education Alliance
Worldwide Disability Solutions
Group**
20525 Mariani Ave., 36SE
Cupertino, CA 95014
(408) 974-7910

These are two of Apple's projects
providing information and technical
assistance about Apple computer
technologies appropriate to meet the
Special Education and Rehabilitation needs of people with a wide
range of disabilities.

**Applied Science and Engineering
Laboratories**
A. I. duPont Institute
P.O. Box 269
Wilmington, DE 19899
(302) 651-6830

Applied Science and Engineering
Laboratories (ASEL) is devoted to
research, development and dissemination of new technologies for people with disabilities. The staff of
ASEL brings expertise from a variety
of disciplines including engineering,
computer science, speech pathology
and psychology. Projects address a
wide range of disability areas united
by the common thread of human-
machine interaction.

**Architectural and Transporation
Barriers Compliance Board
(ATBCB)**
1111 18th St., NW, Suite 501
Washington, DC 20036-3894
(202) 653-7834 (Voice/TDD)
(800) 872-2253 (Voice/TDD)

Assistive Devices Division
Electronics Industries Association
2001 Pennsylvania Ave., N.W.
Washington, DC 20006-1813
(202) 457-8700

The Assistive Device Division is a division within the Electronics Industries Association (Consumer Electronics Group). The purpose of ADD is to promote public awareness of technological solutions to the needs of disabled persons by providing information and educational programs. Other programs include support of legislative initiatives toward funding of technology and development of alternative financing programs for technology for disabled persons.

Association for Retarded Citizens (ARC)
500 E. Border St., 3rd Fl.
Arlington, TX 76010
(817) 640-0204, (800) 433-5255

ARC is a national grassroots organization with over 160,000 members and 1300 chapters covering 48 states. Activities include training volunteers to work with mentally retarded persons; developing demonstration models in areas of education, training and residence; and furthering employment opportunities. Contact ARC for subscription to their newsletter, *the arc* for referral to state and local chapters, and for information about model programs or training centers.

Association of Higher Education Facilities Officers (APPA)
1446 Duke St.
Alexandria, VA 22314
(703) 684-1446

APPA (formerly Association of Physical Plant Administrators) is an international association whose purpose is to promote excellence in the administration, care, operation, planning, and development of higher education facilities. Regional

directors throughout the country can provide referrals to speakers on the topic of accessibility in educational facilities.

Association of Persons in Supported Employment (APSE)
P.O. Box 27523
Richmond, VA 23261
(804) 266-6950

APSE was formed primarily to provide support and information to people who implement supported employment such as job coaches, enclave and mobile crew supervisors, small business entrepreneurs, and program managers. The staff searches for integrated employment opportunities for citizens with severe disabilities by maintaining a partnership of the various participants in Supported Employment. Members receive *The Advance,* the APSE newsletter. They are periodically notified about training opportunities, policy changes, and legislative issues.

Association of Radio Reading Service, Inc.
1010 Vermont Ave., NW, Suite 1100
Washington, DC 20005
(202) 347-0955, (800) 255-2777

More than 100 closed-circuit radio stations throughout the USA broadcast daily news, features, magazine articles, and other programs designed for persons who are print-handicapped, regardless of the disability. These stations provide day and night programming, sometimes 24 hours per day. Many issue printed schedules of their programs. The entire service, including a specially-built radio receiver, is free. To locate the nearest radio reading service, call or write.

Association of Rehabilitation Programs in Data Processing
Center for Information Resources
Philadelphia, PA 19104-3054
(215) 898-8108

This organization offers nationwide data processing training to disabled people. It is dedicated to providing data processing as a career path for persons with a disability and to establish standards and procedures for programs to ensure the maximum benefit for disabled persons.

Association on Handicapped Student Service Programs in Postsecondary Education (AHSSPPE)
P.O. Box 21192
Columbus, OH 43221
(614) 488-4972 (Voice/TDD)

AHSSPPE is a national non-profit organization of members from over 600 institutions of higher education. It promotes full participation of individuals with disabilities in college life. Information sharing is a key element of the goal to upgrade the quality of services available to students with disabilities. Membership benefits include annual conferences, the bimonthly newsletter, *Alert,* and a membership directory. AHSSPPE also sponsors special interest groups, including: Blindness/Visual Impairment, Career Counseling, Community Colleges, Deafness/Hearing Impairment, Head Injury, Learning Disabilities, Minority Issues, TRIO programs, Women and Disability, Canadian Programs, Computers, Disability Studies, and Independent Colleges. It has task forces on AIDS and on Psychiatric Disability.

Ausilioteca
A.I.A.S. Bologna

Via D. Martinelli
18-40133 Bologna, IT 40133
39-51-386516

Ausilioteca is an organization that provides technical and scientific support to requests for aids for the autonomy of disabled people. The group is particularly interested in communication problems, environmental control, and toys and games. The activity of the group is focused in several areas: acquisition of hardware and software materials; consultation; adaptation, personalization and modification of devices; research; and information dissemination.

Autism Society of America
8601 Georgia Ave., Suite 503
Silver Spring, MD 20910
(301) 565-0433

The Society is dedicated to the education and welfare of persons with severe disorders of communication and behavior. With about 200 local chapters and state societies, it is a resource to people across the country. Its Information and Referral Service, list of books, and periodical reprints about autism are available through the national office which invites *written* requests for specific information and referral. Its quarterly membership newsletter is *The Advocate.*

BCI
Easter Seal Communication Institute
250 Ferrand Dr., Suite 200
Don Mills, ON M3C 3P2
(416) 421-8377 × 2313

This organization is dedicated to the development and dissemination of Blissymbolics as a communication system for nonspeaking people. Blissymbols are used in augmentative and assistive communication devices.

Bioengineering Program
Association for Retarded Citizens
250 Ave. J
Arlington, TX 76006
(800) 433-5255

This is a program to apply contemporary technological advances for individuals with mental retardation. It has two major goals: (1) to evaluate currently available technology, and (2) to develop new assistive devices and systems to address unmet needs.

BIPED Corporation
Business Information Processing
   Education for the Disabled
26 Palmer's Hill Rd.
Stanford, CT 06902
(203) 324-3935

This group teaches computer programming to physically disabled individuals at two different locations (Stanford, CT, and White Plains, NY). The courses are available tuition free to disabled individuals.

Blinded Veterans Association
477 H St., NW
Washington, DC 20001
(202) 371-8880

The Blinded Veterans Association is an organization specifically established to promote the welfare of blinded veterans. The association helps by searching out and targeting blinded veterans and their families who need services, assessing their overall needs and linking them to appropriate benefits, services, training and job opportunities.

Braille Institute
741 N. Vermont Ave.

Los Angeles, CA 90029
(213) 663-1111

This institute acts as a technological resource center for both visually and physically disabled individuals.

Canadian Association of Disability Communicators (CADC)
Kimber, Lorne
#52, 8280 Number Two Rd.
Richmond, BC V7C 4P3
(604) 277-8125

The Canadian Association of Disability Communicators (CADC) is a synergistic association of professionals and non-professionals dedicated to the expansion of positive awareness, understanding, acceptance, and integration of people with disabilities.

The Carroll Center for the Blind
770 Centre St.
Newton, MA 02158-2597
(617) 969-6200

This nonprofit organization is dedicated to helping blind and visually impaired individuals. A variety of educational courses are offered, including computer training (Project Cable).

CAST
39 Cross St.
Peabody, MA 01960
(508) 531-8555

This nationally recognized organization researches, develops and disseminates software tools, implementation models, and training techniques for the use of computers to equalize opportunities for children and adults with disabilities. Current focus is Equal Access to education. CAST provides assessments, consultations, and training services for individuals with disabilities, parents, and teachers from across the country. Individualized services can be designed according to interests and needs. Specializations include: Children with learning disabilities and multiple physical handicaps and use of the Macintosh as a tool for mainstreaming children with disabilities.

Center for Computer Assistance to the Disabled (C-CAD)
R.E.A.C.H.
Independent Living Center
Fort Worth, TX 76104
(817) 870-9082
This is an organization that provides computer training and job placement for disabled persons.

Center for Computing and Disability
State University of New York at Albany
Center for Computing and Disability
Albany, NY 12222
(518) 442-3874
The Center for Computing and Disability is currently educating students in the use and adaptation of computing hardware and software. The Center serves people with disabilities from outside the university environment. The Center is broadly concerned with computing.

Center for Psychiatric Rehabilitation
Psychiatric Rehabilitation Services Center
Boston University
730 Commonwealth Ave.
Boston, MA 02215
(617) 353-3550
The Center for Psychiatric Rehabilitation has been jointly funded since 1979 as a Research and Train-

ing Center (RTC) by the National Institute of Mental Health (NIMH). The mission of the Center is to increase knowledge, to train treatment personnel, to develop effective rehabilitation programs, and to assist in organizing both personnel and programs into efficient and coordinated service delivery systems. The Center is organized into three divisions: Research and Training, Technology, and Services. Resource materials related to psychiatric rehabilitation are available upon request.

Center for Special Education Technology and Special Education Software Center
Council for Exceptional Children
1920 Association Dr.
Reston, VA 22091-1589
(703) 620-3660, (703) 264-9463
(800) 873-8255
The Center for Special Education Technology is a federally funded national exchange designed to promote appropriate use of computer, video, and audio technology in special education and to provide information services to educators, parents, product developers, publishers, and others interested in technology for special education. The Center's Hotline number is (800) 873-TALK. Its SpecialNet ID is TECH.CENTER. Information areas include effective and emerging educational practices using technology; hardware and software applications appropriate for special education; current research and advances in technology; national, state and local technology special education resources; viability of the special education market; current product availability; product development and marketing issues;

annual invitational symposium for researchers, and annual invitational technology use meetings.

Center for Technology
Delaware Learning Resource System (DLRS)
102 Willard Hall; U of Delaware
Newark, DE 19716
(302) 451-2084

The Center for Technology provides information on new technologies in the area of special education with the major emphasis on computers and assistive devices. The center houses equipment for diagnostic and prescriptive services. Inservice training is provided on a year-round basis. The center also has a hardware and software lending library.

Center for Technology in Human Disabilities
The Johns Hopkins University
Education Division
Baltimore, MD 21218
(301) 338-8273

The Center promotes the development and use of microcomputers and other technological advances to enable disabled individuals in Maryland and throughout the country to become more independent at home, school, and work. The Center's activities focus on research, training in technology, direct services, and information dissemination.

Center on Postsecondary Education for Students with Learning Disabilities
The University of Connecticut, U-64
249 Glenbrook Rd.
Storrs, CT 06269-2064
(203) 486-4036

The Center offers technical assistance on developing support services for students with learning disabilities for colleges and postsecondary programs throughout the country. Program staff provide training for administrators and postsecondary service providers through inservice presentations and degree programs on campus. In addition, Center staff are involved in on-going research and writing/dissemination on issues related to postsecondary students with learning disabilities. Each June, the Center sponsors the National Postsecondary Training Institute for professionals dealing with postsecondary learning disabilities. *The Postsecondary LD Network News,* which includes information on conferences, resources, and "best practices" for service providers, is published three times a year and is available through the Center on a subscription basis.

CITH
Center for Innovation in Teaching the Handicapped
2805 E. 10th St.
Bloomington, IN 47405
(812) 335-5847

CITH disseminates methods and materials to personnel who work with school age handicapped children. Research reports, training packages, instructional materials, and software packages are listed in the Center's directory.

Clearinghouse on Computer Accommodation (COCA)
General Services Administration (GSA)
KGDO, 18th and F. St. N.W., Rm. 2022
Washington, DC 20405
(202) 523-1906

COCA is a technical resource center of the GSA. Its mission is to assist federal employers and employees to extend office automation technologies to employees with disabilities.

Clearinghouse on Disability Information

Office of Special Education and Rehabilitative Services (OSERS)
U.S. Department of Education
Rm. 3132, Switzer Bldg.
Washington, DC 20202-2524
(202) 732-1241

The Clearinghouse responds to inquiries on a wide range of topics. Information is especially strong in the areas of federal funding for programs serving people with disabilities, federal legislation affecting the disability community, and federal programs benefitting people with handicapping conditions. The Clearinghouse staff are knowledgeable about who has information and refers inquirers to appropriate sources.

Closing the Gap, Inc.
P.O. Box 68
Henderson, MN 56044
(612) 248-3294

Closing the Gap offers national and regional conferences, workshops, and training. CTG also operates a bookstore and publishes a newspaper dedicated to the latest in technology for disabled people. Closing the Gap maintains a database of adaptive devices and software used in special education and rehabilitation.

College Board
ATP Services for Handicapped Students
P.O. Box 6226

Princeton, NJ 08541-6226
(609) 771-7137, (609) 771-7150 (Voice/TDD)

Through its Admissions Testing Program, the College Board provides special arrangements to minimize the possible effects of disabilities on test performance. Two plans are available. Plan A (Special Accommodations) is for students with documented hearing, learning, physical, and/or visual disabilities. It permits special test editions, special answer sheets, extended testing time, aids, and flexible test dates. Plan B, which offers extended time only, is for those with documented learning disabilities. Plan B permits additional testing time for the SAT and TSWE (Test of Standard Written English). Call or write for *Information for Students with Special Needs,* or *Information for Counselors and Admissions Officers.*

Communication Aid Manufacturers Association
1022 Heyl Rd.
Wooster, OH 44691
No phone

The Communication Aid Manufacturers Association (CAMA) is an organization of manufacturers of augmentative and alternative communication (AAC) systems marketed in North America. CAMA promotes professional behavior in the development, manufacture and service of augmentative communication systems. The members are committed to advancing the field of augmentative communication through creating an improved awareness of the state of the art of AAC, advancing the knowledge of AAC professionals, manifesting support for organizations in the field of AAC and acting in the best interest of AAC consumers.

CompuPlay
National Lekotek Center
2100 Ridge Ave.
Evanston, IL 60204
(312) 328-0001
CompuPlay provides computer play sessions for parents and children with special needs ages 2–14. Adaptive equipment and quality software are used to allow children to explore, create, play, and learn. CompuPlay provides a software lending library and computer drop-in center.

CompuSpeech
2210 Wilshire Blvd., Suite 188
Santa Monica, CA 90403
(213) 473-0042
CompuSpeech is an organization that specializes in providing computer assisted treatment using specialized software for individuals with traumatic brain injury or stroke. The group provides individualized speech, language and cognitive evaluation and treatment services for all types of communication problems. CompuSpeech also provides assistance to individuals in hardware and software selection and purchase.

COMPUTE ABLE NETWORK
P.O. Box 1706
Portland, OR 97207
(503) 644-2940
This network assists individuals with various disabilities to adapt and utilize the rapid advances in computer technology.

Computer and Information Science Department
University of Massachusetts

A305 Graduate Research Center
Amherst, MA 01003
(413) 545-2744
The department conducts research in the design of single-switch scanning systems. It is involved in the development and application of microcomputer programs for single-switch scanning. Evaluation of software systems for the disabled person are also conducted.

Computer Resource Center
207 N. San Marco Ave.
St. Augustine, FL 32084
(904) 824-1654 × 581
The Computer Resource Center provides computer training and technical support to teachers of blind students and teachers of deaf students.

Computer Users in Speech and Hearing (CUSH)
School of Speech and Hearing Science
Ohio University
Athens, OH 45701
(614) 594-6168
CUSH is an organization of speech pathologists and audiologists involved in the application of computer technology in the communication sciences. Information is exchanged through journals and a software lending library.

Computers to Help People, Inc.
1221 W. Johnson St.
Madison, WI 53719
(608) 257-5917
This center provides disabled people with vocational training in computer operation. Computers to Help People also sells software designed for physically disabled people.

Concepts
Concepts for Independent Living
2203 Airport Way South
Seattle, WA 98134
(206) 343-0670
This organization is dedicated to developing and expanding independent living opportunities for all disabled people.

Connecticut Parent Advocacy Center
Mohegan Community College
Norwich, CT 06360
(203) 886-5250
This organization acts as a referral agency for people needing information about services for handicapped people.

Coordinating Council for Handicapped Children
220 S. State St.
Chicago, IL 60604
(312) 939-3513
This group provides training programs on special education rights and services for parents and professionals.

COPH-2
Committee on Personal Computers and the Handicapped
2030 W. Irving Park Rd.
Chicago, IL 60618
(312) 866-8195
This consumer organization provides information kits, technical consultation, and low cost computer keyguards. It also loans computers and computer adaptors. It publishes Link-And-Go and maintains a telecommunications bulletin board.

Council for Exceptional Children
1920 Association Dr.
Reston, VA 22091-1589

(703) 620-3660, (703) 264-9463, (800) 873-8255
CEC is a major national association of special education teachers, administrators, and university students training to be teachers. It publishes Exceptional Children and Teaching Exceptional Children. CEC has a division oriented to the use of technology in special education — Technology and Media (TAM).

Council for Learning Disabilities (CLD)
P.O. Box 40303
Overland Park, KS 66204
(913) 492-8755
The CLD is a national organization which serves professionals who work with individuals having learning disabilities. It has an interdisciplinary, field-based focus. The organization sponsors an annual international conference and several regional conferences. It publishes the *Learning Disability Quarterly* and the *LD Forum,* produces videotapes on LD issues, and sponsors grants and awards for research and teaching related to learning disabilities.

Council of Citizens with Low Vision International (CCLVI)
1400 N. Drake Rd., #218
Kalamazoo, MI 49007
(616) 381-9566
CCLVI is an advocacy membership organization composed of individuals with low vision, professionals working with low vision, professionals working in the field, and family members of those with partial vision. CCLVI serves as a clearinghouse on low vision and promotes education, research, legislation and the elimination of barriers to the full use of residual vision.

Publications include a pamphlet, *The Council of Citizens with Low Vision: A Vital Alternative for the Partially Sighted* and a quarterly newsletter. A $1000 scholarship is awarded each year to a person (regardless of race, color, ethnic origin, sex or handicap) who is preparing to work in some capacity as a professional in the field of low vision.

Council of State Administrators of Vocational Rehabilitation (CSAVR)
1055 Thomas Jefferson St., NW
Washington, DC 20007
(202) 638-4634
CSAVR is the membership organization of the State directors of vocational rehabilitation programs. A caller can be referred to the appropriate State office for further assistance.

Council on Assistive Devices and Listening Systems (COADLS)
P.O. Box 32227
Washington, DC 20007
No phone
The primary goal of this organization of manufacturers and distributors is to alert the general public to ways in which electronic devices and systems can help hearing impaired persons cope more effectively with their disability.

Cristina Foundation
National Cristina Foundation, Inc.
666 Steamboat Rd.
Greenwich, CT 06830
(800) 274-7846
The Cristina Foundation is an organization that helps individuals with special needs. The Foundation accepts donations of computer systems, computer peripherals and re-lated technologies and makes the donated equipment available to persons who have physical, sensory, or mental impairments.

Cystic Fibrosis Foundation
6931 Arlington Rd.
Bethesda, MD 20814
(301) 951-4422, (800) 344-4823
The Foundation exists to assure the development of the means to control and prevent cystic fibrosis, and to improve the quality of life for people with the disease. It supports research; accredits a network of Care Centers nationwide; develops materials to help patients, families and the public to understand cystic fibrosis; and seeks to affect public policy.

Direct Link
P.O. Box 6762
Santa Barbara, CA 93160-9942
(805) 964-5708
Direct Link is a non-profit information referral service that links individuals with disability with providers of direct services. Direct Link provides resources for computer technology and training programs.

Disabled Living Centre
Disabled Living Service
Redbank House
Cheetham, Manchester M8 8QA
No phone
The Disabled Living Centre takes the form of a standing exhibition where equipment covering a whole range of disabilities may be examined and demonstrated. The Centre's function is to provide information or advice about equipment to persons with disabilities.

Disabled Programmers, Inc. (DPI)
P.O. Box 23118
San Jose, CA 95153
(408) 629-3700

DPI is an organization that trains disabled individuals to become computer programmers. DPI's Micro Applications Development Lab develops and designs adaptive devices.

Disabled Specialist Group
BCS Disability Program
City University; Dept. CCS;
   Walmsley
London, England EC1V 2PA
(071) 251-4073

The British Computer Society maintains a disability special interest group. The purpose of the Disabled Specialist Group is to identify and promote ways technology can effectively improve the quality of life of people with disabilities, disseminate information, provide disabled people with the opportunity to make technology work for them and to influence manufacturers in the design of their equipment.

**Disabled Veterans of America
   (DAV)**
807 Maine Ave., SW
Washington, DC 20024
(202) 554-3501

DAV is a national membership organization of service-oriented disabled veterans, their families, and survivors. Its National Service Program (NSO) advises members and non-members across the country. Without charge, DAV NSOs act as advocates for individuals to obtain the benefits to which they are entitled. DAV works to lower the rate of unemployment among disabled veterans and the level of discrimination against them. The Voluntary

Service Program (VAVS) operates nationwide, as does the Transportation Network.

**East Range Developmental
   Achievement Center, Inc.**
800 A. Ave.
Eveleth, MN 55734
(218) 744-5130

This center is for the exchange of information on the use of microcomputers by persons with developmental disabilities.

Easter Seal Systems
The National Easter Seal Society
Chicago, IL 60612
(312) 667-7400

This organization sponsors grants for software development for disabled persons and is developing regional adaptive device centers. Provides education, training, and discounts on selected computer systems.

Educational Equity Concepts Resource Center
114 E. 32 St.
New York, NY 10016
(212) 725-1803

The Resource Center furthers educational opportunities for women and girls with disabilities by systematically collecting information and making it available to educational institutions and organizations as well as to individuals. A database is being created and a Guide to Educational Services will result. It is a project of the Women's Educational Equity Act Program of the U.S. Department of Education.

Educational Resources Information Center (ERIC)

ERIC is an information system providing access to journal and

document literature dealing with education in 16 specialized areas including: higher education; adult, career and vocational education; tests, measurement and evaluation; rural education and small schools; reading and communications skills; science, mathematics and environmental education; handicapped and gifted children; and teacher education. Entries are all annotated, and many can be obtained on microfiche or paper copy reproduction through ERIC. Reprints of most articles can be obtained through University Microfilms International. A computer search of the ERIC database can be made by subject. To access the system, go to one of the 800 subscribing libraries found throughout the country, or seek further information at the nearest college or university library. If unable to find information there, contact:
ERIC Clearinghouse on Higher Education
George Washington University
One Dupont Circle, NW, Suite 630
Washington, DC 20036, (202) 296-2597; or
ERIC Clearinghouse on Handicapped and Gifted Children, 1920 Association Dr., Reston, VA 22091, (703) 620-3660.

The Electronic University
TeleLearning Systems, Inc.
505 Beach St.
San Francisco, CA 94133
(415) 928-2800
The Electronic University offers home courses (including tutoring) on personal improvement, business and professional skills, and credit/degree programs via computers. It also provides counseling, an electronic library, and a seminar series.

Epilepsy Foundation of America
4351 Garden City Dr.
Landover, MD 20785
(301) 459-3700, (800) 332-1000 (Consumers), (800) 322-4050 (Professional Library)
The Foundation and its local affiliates support many programs of information, referral, public and professional education, employment assistance, advocacy and self-help. The Foundation publishes pamphlets, brochures, a 12-page newsletter, and offers a membership program. The National Epilepsy Library provides technical information services to professionals. The national office also provides patient information and referral, supports medical research, works with government agencies, and works with Congress to advance the interests of people with epilepsy.

Estate Planning for the Disabled (EPD)
955 W. Center Ave., Suite #12
Manteca, CA 95336
(209) 239-7558, (800) 448-1071
EPD is a national corporation the purpose of which is to counsel and assist parents of special needs children to develop (at the lowest possible cost) viable estate plans, letters of intent, wills, and special needs trusts. Estate teams consisting of a planner, attorney, and a CPA have been organized in several California locations and elsewhere in the country. Special payment plans and discounts are available to low-income families. Seminars, workshops, and resource lists are among the services offered. EPD has 58 offices in 34 states to provide local assistance. Callers from other states will be assisted or referred to appropriately

trained and experienced attorneys and financial specialists.

Family Survival Project
425 Bush St.; Suite 500
San Francisco, CA 94108
(415) 434-3388
　　The Family Survival Project is an organization concerned with the problems that arise when an adult acquires a chronic, traumatic, permanent or progressive brain disorder. The project provides counseling, respite care, self-help support groups and education for families and advocates. Publications and training materials are available nationally.

Federation for Children with Special Needs
312 Stuart St.
Boston, MA 02116
(617) 482-2915
　　This coalition of parent organizations offers technical assistance and resource information on children with various disabilities.

Federation of the Handicapped, Inc.
211 W. 14th St.
New York, NY 10011
(212) 242-9050
　　The Federation trains disabled individuals in word processing and general education.

FIGHT, Inc. Library
Family Interest Group—Head Trauma, Inc. Library
1370 Wellesley Ave.
St. Paul, MN 55105
(612) 478-6477
　　This group offers advice, information, and materials (for a returnable deposit) on head trauma, rehabilita-

tion, medical care, and adaptive lifestyles.

Foundation Center
79 Fifth Ave.
New York, NY 10003
(212) 620-4230
　　The Center operates four libraries (in New York, Washington, DC, Cleveland, and San Francisco). In these, and various other libraries across the country, are found four reference books which index foundations and grants made to organizations serving persons with disabilities. In a few cases, grants to individuals are listed. To find the address of the nearest of the 150 collections, call the New York number above.

Foundation for Science and the Handicapped (FSH)
1141 Iroquois Dr. #114
Naperville, IL 60563
　　FSH is an organization of scientists and professionals in various fields, many of whom have disabilities, who offer their skills to help solve disability-related problems. Inquirers will be referred to members who can respond to requests for guidance, problem clarification, or career suggestions. Members assist educational institutions and industry to create favorable conditions for people with disabilities. They also publish a book by S. P. Stearner, *Able Scientists—Disabled Persons* ($12.95). Some grants are available to disabled students who are: college seniors or beyond; already accepted or enrolled in graduate or professional school; and are in science, mathematics or engineering. (Send requests for information on grants to: Rebecca F. Smith, 115 S.

Brainard Ave., LaGrange, IL
60625.)

Gazette International Networking Institute (GINI)

4502 Maryland Ave.
St. Louis, MO 63108
(314) 361-0475

GINI seeks to reach, inform and dignify people with disabilities throughout the world through its network of people and publications. *Rehabilitation Gazette* is an international journal written by individuals with a disability, is published biannually and contains articles and resources pertinent to disability.

Polio Network News, published quarterly, contains updated information on the late effects of polio. GINI also publishes an annual *Post-Polio Directory* which lists clinics, health professionals, and support groups. *I.V.U.N. News,* for ventilator users, is published biannually and contains the latest information on home mechanical ventilation. There is a modest fee for the publications and questions are welcome.

Gray's Book Company

1821 Solano Ave.
Berkeley, CA 94707
(415) 527-9677

Gray's Book Company is a family-owned bookstore with mail order services. The company offers a selection of materials of particular interest to parents of disabled children and to teachers, medical personnel, other caregivers and all those in the fields touched by special needs.

Handicapped Access Center

Duluth Public Library
520 W. Superior St.
Duluth, MN 55802
(218) 723-3809

The Center trains disabled persons in the use of the Apple IIe. Applications include word processing, database, Applesoft Basic, Logo, etc. Product information on software, hardware, and adaptations is available.

Hear You Are, Inc. (HYAI)

4 Musconetcong Ave.
Stanhope, NJ 07874
(201) 347-7662 (Voice/TDD)

HYAI provides assistance with assistive technology devices for people who are deaf or hard of hearing. Devices available through a mail order catalogue include FM systems, telephone and doorbell devices, television amplifiers, smoke-alert devices, hearing protection, infrared systems, closed captioning devices and more. Videotapes, therapy activities, motivational rewards, and books on hearing-related subjects are also available. Schools and businesses may request workshops on subjects related to hearing impairment.

HEATH Resource Center

1 Dupont Circle
Washington, DC 20036-1193
(202) 939-9320

The federally funded HEATH Resource Center (Higher Education and the Handicapped) operates the National Clearinghouse on Postsecondary Education for Handicapped Individuals. Major emphasis is in the area of computer applications.

Helen Keller National Center for Deaf-Blind Youths and Adults (HKNC)

111 Middle Neck Rd.
Sands Point, NY 11050
(516) 944-8900 (Voice/TDD)

The Helen Keller National Center provides diagnostic evaluation, short-term comprehensive rehabilitation and personal adjustment training, job preparation and placement for deaf-blind youths and adults 18 years of age and older. It conducts an extensive network of field services through regional offices, affiliate programs, and a National Training Team. There is a Technical Assistance Center headquartered in the New York office. It offers services for elderly deaf-blind persons and has a National Parent and Family service project. Publications include the *HKNC TAC News.*

Hotline to Educational Data
Educational Research and Improvement
U.S. Department of Education
Washington, DC 20208
(800) 424-1616
The U.S. Dept. of Ed. has established an "800" number to help identify data, research or reports on any aspect of special education. The toll-free hotline provides a good starting point.

IBM National Support Center for Persons with Disabilities
4111 Northside Pkwy.
Atlanta, GA 30327
(800) 426-2133, (800) 284-9482 (TDD)
The Center responds to requests for information on how computers can help people with a wide range of disabilities to use personal computers. While the Center is unable to diagnose or prescribe an assistive device of software, free information is provided on what is available and where one can go for more details.

ICD — International Center for the Disabled
340 E. 24th St.
New York, NY 10010
(212) 679-0100, (212) 889-0372 (TDD)
ICD is a comprehensive outpatient rehabilitation facility offering half-day to two-week professional education courses/workshops on a broad range of medical and vocational evaluation, day treatment for dementia, cognitive rehabilitation for head injury survivors and learning disabilities. A catalogue of offerings is available.

Immune Deficiency Foundation (IDF)
P.O. Box 586
Columbia, MD 21045
(301) 461-3127
The goal of the IDF is to promote increased research, medical training, and public education on and for the primary immune deficiency disorders. Through a national office and several regional chapters, the Foundation has developed programs for patients and parents, professional education, research support, and legislative interaction. Its focus is on the genetic, primary immunodeficiency diseases (rather than on others such as AIDS and Multiple Sclerosis). Affiliate groups can be found in California, Florida, Illinois, Missouri, New England, Ohio, Oklahoma, Texas and Utah.

Independent Living Research Utilization Program (ILRU)
3400 Bissonnet, Suite 101
Houston, TX 77005
(713) 666-6244 (Voice), (713) 666-0643 (TDD)
ILRU Program is a national resource center for independent living, and is a federally funded research and training center on improving

effectiveness in independent living centers. It produces resource materials, develops and conducts training programs on independent living issues, provides technical assistance and consultation to independent living centers, conducts a variety of research projects on factors affecting independence, and publishes a bimonthly newsletter which addresses matters affecting the independent living field. The major resource is the *Directory of Independent Living Programs,* which lists programs on a state-by-state basis ($8.50 prepaid). Individuals are invited to contact ILRU for free referral to projects near their communities. Write for complete publications list.

Information Resource Center
The Center for Rehabilitation Technology Services
1410-C Boston Ave.
P.O. Box 15
West Columbia, SC 29171-0015
(803) 739-5362
The Information Resource Center provides information on assistive technology. Materials at the center include books and reports on different types of assistive technology, reference guides and directories, product literature, conference proceedings, journals and periodicals in the field and video tapes on commercial products and service delivery programs.

Information Technology Center (ITC)
Department of Veterans Affairs (VA)
Central Office, Rm. 237
810 Vermont Ave., NW
Washington, DC 20420
(202) 233-5524
The Information Technology

Center provides computer training programs for the Veterans Administration and other federal employees with disabilities, especially for individuals with vision limitations. Reference literature concerning products and other clearinghouse contacts is maintained. The listed telephone line is open to any individual requesting reference information, hot line support and upfront consulting for initial guidance. The center also sponsors demonstrations that are open to any interested individual.

INNOTEK
National Lekotek Center
2100 Ridge Ave.
Evanston, IL 60204
(312) 328-0001
INNOTEK is the technology division of the National Lekotek Center. The division provides technology-related resources to families and to special education professionals throughout the country. INNOTEK provides multidimensional technology resources that include: teacher training and consultation to school districts, therapy centers, and recreational programs. INNOTEK is also working to expand the nationwide network of COMPUPLAY Centers. The INNOTEK staff is also able to provide graduate level training courses to professionals as well as custom training courses for agencies.

Institute on Alcohol, Drugs and Disability (IADD)
2165 Bunker Hill Dr.
San Mateo, CA 94402
(415) 578-8047 (Voice/TDD)
IADD addresses the fact that people with disabilities frequently are chemically dependent, or they are at

risk of becoming dependent. The organization advocates to increase the accessibility of alcohol and other drug abuse prevention and treatment programs that do exist and to increase the number available. It has conducted the California Alcohol, Drug and Disability Study (CALADDS), which generated data and recommendations for improving accessibility to the California alcohol and drug service system. Quarterly, the Coalition publishes *The Seed* to inform professionals and consumers about the connection between alcohol, drugs, and disability. The Institute is organizing a national policy development and leadership symposium (July–August 1991) and will publish a proceedings of that event. The organization provides technical assistance to all interested in improving access to care and prevention services.

ISAAC
International Society for Augmentative and Alternative Communication
P.O. Box 1762
Toronto, ON M4G 4A3
(416) 424-3806
    This information and referral organization is for individuals concerned about and/or working in the area of communication disorders. It publishes Communication Outlook.

Jewish Hospital — Occupational Therapy Department
216 S. Kings Hwy.
St. Louis, MO 63110
(314) 454-7752

Job Accommodation Network (JAN)
West Virginia University
809 Allen Hall

Morgantown, WV 26506
(304) 293-7186, (800) 526-7234
    JAN is an international information network and consulting resource which provides information about employment issues to employers, rehabilitation professionals, and persons with disabilities. Callers should be prepared to explain the specific problem and job circumstances. Sponsored by President's Committee on Employment of People with Disabilities, the Network is operated by West Virginia University Rehabilitation Research and Training Center. Brochures, printed materials, and a newsletter are available free of charge.

Job Opportunities for the Blind (JOB)
National Federation of the Blind
1800 Johnson St.
Baltimore, MD 21230
(301) 659-9314, (800) 638-7518
    JOB is the nationwide job listing and job referral system of the NFB, a service available without charge. JOB has more than 40 free publications, among which are: *Blind People at Work,* and *Technical Assistance Guide for Employers.* The *Recorded Bulletin* is sent to registered applicants and includes articles about careers and employment, as well as job listing.

Johns Hopkins University — Education Division
The Johns Hopkins University
Education Division
Baltimore, MD 21218
(301) 338-8273
    Johns Hopkins offers both a Masters and a Doctoral program in Special Education Technology. The Education Division conducts re-

search on integrating microcomputers into the special education classroom.

L.D. College Writers Project
University of Minnesota
216 Pillsbury Dr. S.E.
Minneapolis, MN 55455
(612) 376-1672
   Training and practice in word processing is provided to college level learning disabled writers. A set of papers on compiled research is distributed by mail at cost.

Learning Disabilities Network
25 Accord Park Dr.
Rockland, MA 02370
(617) 982-8100
   The Network provides educational and referral services for learning-disabled individuals, their families, and professionals, primarily in the Northeast. Available on a nationwide basis are printed materials about learning disabilities. The Network also offers conferences, seminars, and workshops. *The Exchange,* a semiannual newsletter, is free to members and $20/year to nonmembers. The Network Scholarship Fund for Individuals with Learning Disabilities makes quality educational therapy more accessible.

Learning Disability Association of America
4156 Library Rd.
Pittsburgh, PA 15234
(412) 341-1515
   This organization of professionals and parents is devoted to advancing the education and well-being of children and adults with learning disabilities. A learning disability could result from perceptual or conceptual problems. The disability is sometimes accompanied by behavior problems.

Life Services for the Handicapped, Inc.
352 Park Ave. South
New York, NY 10010
(212) 532-6740
   Life Services is a national non-profit organization which helps families address issues in longterm planning for their members with severe disability. Through partnerships with a wide variety of local organizations, and some direct service, arrangements are made to utilize available resources. The goal is a high quality of life, without the loneliness and isolation so common in later years.

LIFT, Inc.
350 Pfingsten
Northbrook, IL 60062
(312) 564-9005
   This organization offers help in training and hiring handicapped individuals as computer programmers. LIFT has used a five-step process model to help data processing, engineering, and human resources executives to identify, train, and hire skilled and dedicated entry-level computer professionals with physical disabilities.

Madalaine Pugliese Associates, Inc.
5 Bessom St.
Suite 175
P.O. Box 4000
Marblehead, MA 01945-4000
(617) 639-1930
   Madalaine Pugliese Associates, Inc. conducts adaptive technology seminars and conferences throughout the United States and Canada. The goal of the group is to support the advancement of microcomputer applications for disabled individuals. The group offers formal courses and

hands-on workshops for individuals and organizations which seek to apply adaptive technology in support of disabled clients, students and employees.

Mainstream, Inc.
1030 15th St., NW, Suite 1010
Washington, DC 20005
(202) 898-1400 (Voice/TDD)

This nonprofit organization works with employers and service providers around the country to increase employment opportunities for persons with disabilities. Mainstream produces publications and provides in-house training, conferences and technical assistance on complying with the Americans with Disabilities Act. Mainstream operates its own placement programs in Washington, DC, and Dallas, TX.

**Maryland Rehabilitation Center —
Technology Resource Center**
2301 Argonne Dr.
Baltimore, MD 21218
(301) 366-8800 × 231

This resource center provides evaluation of computer applications best suited for enhancing a disabled person's vocation. It acts as a diagnostic resource center in setting disabled students' vocational goals.

**Massachusett's Rehabilitation
Commission Library**
22th Fl., Statler Office Bldg.
Boston, MA 02116
(617) 727-1140

This library is dedicated exclusively to literature about disabled people. Information about computers and adaptive devices is available free of charge to individuals who are disabled.

Missouri LINC
Department of Special Education
and Practical Arts & Vocational-
Technical Education
609 Maryland St.
Columbia, MO 65211
(314) 882-2733

This state funded special education program is for teachers of handicapped students ages 3–21. Offerings include a newsletter and a Bulletin Board (on SpecialNet) that provides information on assistive devices.

**Mobility International, USA
(MIUSA)**
P.O. Box 3551
Eugene, OR 97403
(503) 343-1284 (Voice/TDD)

MIUSA is the American office of the London-based organization founded in 1973 to integrate persons with disabilities into international educational exchange programs and travel. It offers members information and referral services. It has sponsored programs to Costa Rica, Germany, England, China, and the Soviet Union. Publications include: *You Want to Go Where? — A Guide to China for Persons with Disabilities* ($9.95), *Global Perspectives on Disability — Curriculum, A World of Options for the 1990's: A Guide to International Educational Exchange, Community Services, and Travel for Persons with Disabilities* ($14 members; $16 non-members); *A Manual for Integrating Persons with Disabilities into International Education Exchange Programs* ($16 members; $18 non-members); and *Over the Rainbow,* a quarterly newsletter available to persons/organizations for $10/year. MIUSA also sells two videos which demonstrate the important role that people with disabilities play in international educational exchange and travel ($49 each). These are available in English or Spanish, and with captions for deaf and hard of hearing persons. MIUSA's programs for 1991 include Mexico, China, and the USSR.

Modern Talking Picture Services, Inc. (MTPS)
5000 Park St. North
St. Petersburg, FL 33709
(813) 545-8781, (800) 237-6213 (Voice/TDD)
This company distributes captioned films and videos for educational and general interest purposes. To obtain an educational film in captioned form, one hearing impaired student must be among the users. To obtain a general interest item, a group of hearing impaired persons is a prerequisite. Contact MTPS for an application.

Music Therapy Association
25 Gelston Ave.
Brooklyn, NY 11209
(718) 745-9231
The Association provides services for disabled people interested in computer generated music systems. Services include consulting and system set-up.

NAHSA
National Association of Hearing and Speech Action
10801 Rockville Pike
Rockville, MD 20852
(301) 897-5700
NAHSA is a consumer advocacy group for speech and hearing impaired persons and deaf persons.

National AIDS Information Clearinghouse (NAIC)
P.O. Box 6003
Rockville, MD 20850
(301) 762-5111, (800) 342-2437, (800) 344-7432 (Spanish), (800) 458-5231 (professionals), (800) 243-7889 (TDD)
NAIC is a comprehensive information service for health professionals, state and local AIDS program managers, and others responsible for reaching the public with AIDS information. Sponsored by the Centers for Disease Control, NAIC maintains the toll-free lines above. Additional materials are available by writing.

National Alliance for the Mentally Ill (NAMI)
2101 Wilson Blvd., Suite 302
Arlington, VA 22201
(703) 524-7600, (800) 950-6264
NAMI is a self-help organization of mentally ill persons, their families, and their friends. Composed of over 1000 affiliate groups, nationwide, its goals are mutual support, education, and advocacy for the victims of severe mental illness. The philosophy is that brain disease causes schizophrenia, manic depressions, and other disabling conditions. Support groups provide coping strategies to families and to the persons with mental illness. Call to get the closest affiliated group. NAMI offers a newsletter, the *NAMI Advocate,* and other publications.

National Alliance of Blind Students (NABS)
1155 15th St., NW, Suite 720
Washington, DC 20005
(202) 467-5081, (800) 424-8666
NABS provides a national voice for students with vision impairments. It has an annual convention;

a national newsletter, *The Student Advocate* ($3/year); and a program to assist with employment. The staff does scholarship searches and is constantly updating its list of opportunities. Membership is $5/year. NABS is an affiliate of the American Council of the Blind.

National Association for the Visually Handicapped (NAVH)
22 W. 21st St.
New York, NY 10010
(212) 889-3141

NAVH offers services for people with partial vision. Information booklets and publications (much in large print) are available for consumers, their families, professionals and paraprofessionals, and for the business community. A free Loan Library of Large Print is available through the mail. Newsletters are issued once or twice a year: *SEEING CLEARLY* for adults and *IN FOCUS* for children (both in large print).

National Association of Protection & Advocacy Systems (NAPAS)
900 Second St., NE, Suite 211
Washington, DC 20002
(202) 408-9514, (202) 408-9521
  (TDD)

NAPAS is the membership association of the directors of three Federally-funded programs: the Protection & Advocacy Systems (P&As) for persons with Developmental Disabilities and the P&As for persons with Mental Illness, which provide legal advocacy for clients; and the Client Assistance Program (CAP), which assists clients of vocational rehabilitation services with eligibility and legal problems. NAPAS provides technical assistance and training for members and staffs,

and it monitors Congressional and Federal agency activities related to disability issues and oversight administration.

National Association of Rehabilitation Facilities
P.O. Box 17675
Washington, DC 20041
(703) 556-8848

National Association of Rehabilitation Facilities is the national voluntary organization representing the interests of facilities serving the needs of disabled persons. It promotes expansion and improvement of rehabilitation services to disabled persons as provided in rehabilitation facilities and provides a mechanism for joint action in this field.

The National Association of the Deaf (NAD)
814 Thayer Ave.
Silver Spring, MD 20910
(301) 587-1788

Functions as a clearinghouse for information on total communication, which includes all forms of communication for people with severe hearing impairment. Major concerns include legal and employment rights of deaf people. Most states have affiliated chapters. The Junior NAD promotes independent living and self-determination especially for secondary and postsecondary students, ages 14–21.

National Association of Vocational Education Special Needs Personnel (NAVESNP)
c/o Athens Technical Institute
U.S. Hwy. 29 N.
Athens, GA 30610
(404) 549-2362

NAVESNP is a membership organization of secondary and post-vocational education professionals concerned with the education of disadvantaged students and students with disabilities or other special needs. The *NAVESNP Journal* is available quarterly to members ($12/year), and there are five regional subgroups which meet in addition to the annual meeting. Consumers, advisers, and parents can obtain local referrals to people qualified to do vocational evaluations.

National Braille Press, Inc.
88 Saint Stephens St.
Boston, MA 02115
(617) 266-6160
This organization publishes books of special interest to blind and vision impaired persons. It publishes books and magazines in braille and provides transcription services for books, magazines, and pamphlets.

National Captioning Institute (NCI)
5203 Leesburg Pike, Suite 1500
Falls Church, VA 22041
(703) 998-2400, (800) 533-9673 (Voice), (800) 321-8337 (TDD)
NCI is a non-profit corporation whose goal is to expand the captioned television service. The staff produces captions for television programs. NCI also designs, manufactures, and distributes the TeleCaption decoder device, which is attached to the user's television set (under $200 each).

National Center for Learning Disabilities (NCLD)
99 Park Ave., 6th Fl.
New York, NY 10016
(212) 687-7211

NCLD helps people affected with this "hidden handicap" to live self-sufficient, productive and fulfilling lives. Services include raising public awareness and understanding; legislative advocacy; information and referrals and special educational programs and products for parents and professionals in this country and abroad. *THEIR WORLD* is an annual magazine with features about children, youth, and adults; it is enhanced by excellent photography and articles about nationwide efforts.

National Center for Youth with Disabilities (NCYD)
Adolescent Health Program
University of Minnesota
Box 721-UMHC
Harvard St. at East River Rd.
Minneapolis, MN 55455
(612) 626-2825, (612) 624-3939 (TDD), (800) 333-6293
NCYD, a collaborative program of the Society for Adolescent Medicine and the Adolescent Health program at the University of Minnesota, is a technical assistance and information resource center focusing on adolescents with chronic illness and disability and the issues that surround their transition to adult life. NCYD's national Resource Library is an on-line computerized database containing interdisciplinary information on current research, model programs, training and educational materials, federal and state law and legislation, and a technical assistance network. The Library's information may be accessed directly with a microcomputer and modem or by calling to request a database search by an information specialist. NCYD's publications include topical annotated bibliographies, *Cydline Reviews;* a

quarterly newsletter, *Connections;* and brief fact sheets.

National Center on Disability Services (NCDS)
201 I.U. Willets Rd.
Albertson, NY 11507
(516) 747-5400, (516) 747-5355 (TDD)

NCDS is a non-profit organization which engages in education, research, vocational counseling, job training and placement for children and adults with disabilities. There are four main divisions: (1) The Henry Viscardi School is for children with severe disabilities (pre K–12 grade); and it has a community program for adult/continuing education which includes some courses for people with disabilities and others where people with and without disabilities learn together. (2) Vocational Rehabilitation Services offers counseling, training and placement of adults with disabilities. (3) Research & Training Institute education, transition from school-to-work, employment and career development of persons with disabilities. (4) Abilities, Health, and Rehabilitation Services runs an outpatient service. Copies of the annual report and other information is available upon request.

National Center on Employment of the Deaf
National Technical Institute for the Deaf
1 Lomb Memorial Dr.
Rochester, NY 14623
(716) 475-6400

The National Center on Employment of the Deaf provides information and consulting services to deaf and hearing impaired job seekers, professionals working with hearing impaired people and employers and potential employers of hearing impaired people. They provide information, training and consultation on innovative job placement techniques, employee selection, safety, communications, insurance, driving and tax benefits.

National Chronic Pain Outreach Association, Inc. (NCPOA)
7979 Old Georgetown Rd., Suite 100
Bethesda, MD 20814-2429
(301) 652-4948

NCPOA is a non-profit organization whose purpose is to disseminate information about chronic pain and its management. They operate an information clearinghouse which publishes a quarterly newsletter, *Lifeline;* sponsors public information efforts; and develops local support groups for people with chronic pain and their families. Low-cost pamphlets, publications, and audio- and video-cassette tapes are available.

National Clearinghouse for Professions in Special Education
Information Center
c/o Council for Exceptional Children
1920 Association Dr.
Reston, VA 22091
(703) 264-9475, (703) 620-3660 (TDD)

The Professions Clearinghouse is designed to encourage individuals to seek careers in the various fields related to the education of children and youth with disabilities. The Clearinghouse collects, synthesizes, and disseminates information regarding career opportunities, personnel supply and demand, and personnel preparation programs for increasing the supply of qualified professionals serving individuals with disabilities. The Clearinghouse also provides information, technical assistance, and linkages to promote local, state, and national efforts to collect useful information in these areas.

National Clearinghouse of Rehabilitation Training Materials
Oklahoma State University
Stillwater, OK 74078
(405) 624-5000

This clearinghouse disseminates research papers, monographs, and training manuals to meet the information needs of rehabilitation practitioners throughout the United States.

National Committee for Citizens in Education (NCCE)
10840 Little Patuxent Pkwy., Suite 301
Columbia, MD 21044-3199
(301) 997-9300, (800) 638-9675

NCCE is an organization devoted to improving the quality of public schools through increased public involvement. It provides information resources to parents and citizens for decision-making at the local level. A toll-free help line is available to parents, 10 a.m. to 5 p.m. (EST). English and Spanish counselors are available. The newsletter, *Network,* appears 6 times per year; the Summer, 1988 issue featured disability-related technology resources. An "Access Printout" called *College Opportunities for Learning Disabled Students,* a catalogue, and a price list are available.

National Council on Disability
800 Independence Ave., SW, Suite 814
Washington, DC 20591
(202) 267-3846 (Voice), (202) 267-3232 (TDD)

The National Council is an independent federal agency comprised of 15 members appointed by the President and confirmed by the Senate. It is charged with addressing, analyzing, and making recommendations on issues of public policy which affect people with disabilities. The National Council originated and developed the first draft of the Americans with Disabilities Act, which was signed into law by President Bush on July 26, 1990. The National Council distributes a free newsletter, *FOCUS,* and welcomes requests for copies of policy papers. Publications include *On the Threshold of Independence (1988), An Assessment of Federal Laws and Programs Affecting Persons with Disabilities — Legislative Recommendations* (no cost).

National Council on Independent Living (NCIL)
310 S. Peoria St., Suite 201
Chicago, IL 60607
(312) 226-1006 (Voice/TDD)

NCIL is a national membership association for independent living centers and supporters. It disseminates information about independent living matters and relevant legislation through its membership network. It can provide referral to a local program for consumers, up-to-date practical information for professionals, and advice to persons interested in starting an independent living center.

National Down Syndrome Congress
1800 Dempster
Park Ridge, IL 60068
(312) 823-7550

This organization of parents and professionals provides information on services for persons with Down Syndrome.

National Easter Seal Society
70 East Lake St.
Chicago, IL 60601
(312) 726-6200, (312) 726-4258
  (TDD)

1350 New York Ave., NW
Washington, DC 20005
(202) 347-3066
   The National Easter Seal Society is a nonprofit, community-based health agency dedicated to increasing the independence of people with disabilities. Easter Seals offers a wide range of quality services, research and programs to assist adults and children with disabilities and their families. The centers offer employment opportunities for physical, occupational, speech, and other rehabilitation professionals. The Washington office monitors federal legislation and regulations, and it publishes a quarterly newsletter *Washington Watch Line.* A publication list is available.

National Federation of the Blind
1800 Johnson St.
Baltimore, MD 21230
(301) 659-9314
   This membership organization with more than 500 state and local chapters in the U.S. focuses on self-help for blind persons, public rights, and current information. The group publishes the *Braille Monitor.*

National Federation of the Blind, Student Division
31548 Large Vista Rd.
Valley Center, CA 92082
(619) 749-0103
   The Student Division of the NFB

is an organization dedicated to considering and acting upon issues of concern to blind students. With affiliates in over twenty states, this division provides a nationwide network for blind students. The Student Division is a self-support network for blind students and a mechanism for political action. Serving as the collective voice of organized blind students in America, the Student Division meets on a continuing basis with such major service providers as Recording for the Blind and the Educational Testing Service. Its purpose is to change "what it means to be a blind student in America."

National Head Injury Foundation
333 Turnpike Rd.
Southborough, MA 01772
(508) 485-9950
   The National Head Injury Foundation is an organization of families, consumers, professionals and other advocates. The goals are to make the public aware of the high incidence of head injury and to provide programs and services to meet the needs of head injury survivors.

National Health Information Center
O.D.P.H.P.
P.O. Box 1133
Washington, DC 20013-1133
(800) 336-4797
   The Information Center welcomes inquiries from consumers and professionals interested in health-related disability issues. Referrals are provided to appropriate organizations. It is a service of the U.S. Department of Health and Human Services' Office of Disease Prevention and Health Promotion. Publications include: *Health Information Resources*

in Federal Government; *Staying Healthy:*
A Bibliography of Health Promotion
Materials, and Health Finders such as:
Selected Federal Health Information
Clearinghouses and *Information Centers*
and Toll-Free Numbers for Health Infor-
mation (handling fee charged).

**National Home Study Council
(NHSC)**
1601 18th St. NW
Washington, DC 20009
(202) 234-5100
NHSC is a voluntary association
of accredited home study schools,
founded in 1926 to promote sound
educational standards and ethical
business practices within the home
study field. Through its Accrediting
Commission it recognizes nearly 100
schools and centers which sponsor
courses of study that can be accomplished by students on their own.
These may include degree, as well
as non-degree, programs.

**National Information Center for
Children and Youth with
Handicaps**
P.O. Box 1492
Washington, DC 20013
(703) 893-6061
The National Information Center
for Children and Youth with Handicaps provides free information to
assist parents, educators, caregivers,
advocates and others in helping
children and youth with disabilities
become participating members of
the community. The center maintains a database of information on
disability topics for easy access and
dissemination. It has prepackaged
information to respond to frequently
asked questions and to requests for
materials specifically concerned with
children of minority groups and the
people who work with them.

**National Information Center on
Deaf-Blindness**
College Hall 217
800 Florida Ave., NE
Washington, DC 20002
(202) 651-5289
The National Information Center
on Deaf-Blindness is a national
clearinghouse that assists educators,
other professionals and parents by
identifying effective teaching approaches, materials and resources
for deaf-blind children and respond-
ing to inquiries about deaf-blindness.

**National Information Center on
Deafness**
Gallaudet College
Washington, DC 20002
(202) 651-5109
This center provides either direct
information or appropriate references to deaf or hearing impaired
individuals. The Center also publishes brief bibliographies and nar-
rative fact sheets on requested topics
free of charge.

**National Institute for Rehabilita-
tion Engineering (NIRE)**
97 Decker Rd.
Butler, NJ 07405
(201) 853-6585
This organization is an information and referral center for disabled
persons seeking computer oriented
rehabilitation. A multidisciplinary
research, training, and service organization, it provides custom-
designed and custom-made tools and
devices, along with intensive personal task-performance and driver
training.

National Lekotek Center
2100 Ridge Ave.

Evanston, IL 60204
(312) 328-0001

Lekotek serves handicapped children ages 2–14. It provides computer play sessions (Compuplay) for parents and children and has a software lending library for parents. Lekotek uses adaptive equipment and specialized software.

National Library Service for the Blind and Physically Handicapped
Library of Congress
1291 Taylor St., NW
Washington, DC 20542
(202) 707-5100

The Library Service provides, free of charge, recorded and braille reading materials to persons with documented visual or physical impairments which prevent the reading of standard print material. *A Union Catalog* lists 72,000 books currently available in braille or on recordings. Contact the Reference Section with any questions about types of materials needed. Descriptive literature is available.

National Mental Health Association (NMHA)
1021 Prince St.
Alexandria, VA 22314-7722
(703) 684-7722

NMHA has an active information center which can refer callers to one of 600 affiliate centers across the country. It also has fact sheets about various types of mental illness and mental health, such as schizophrenia, depression, adolescent suicide prevention, stress and tension. Its Office of Prevention has curricular materials for elementary, secondary, and college use. Founded in 1909, NMHA develops and urges policy

position on key issues, and trains volunteers in client support services and advocacy. The quarterly newsletter FOCUS is $15/year. Also available is an extensive list of publications.

National Mental Health Consumer Self-Help Clearinghouse
311 S. Juniper St., Suite 902
Philadelphia, PA 19107
(215) 735-2481

This clearinghouse draws upon the experience of many individuals and groups who have extensive experience organizing self-help groups. Topics include fund-raising, press and community relations, advocacy, recruitment, and network-building. Each state has a designated office to do protection and advocacy for mental illness. Call for referral.

National Network of Learning Disabled Adults (NNLDA)
800 N. 82 St.
Scottsdale, AZ 85257
(602) 941-5112

NNLDA is an organization run by and for people who have learning disabilities. A free newsletter and list of self-help groups is available. Please send a stamped envelope for mail responses.

National Organization for Rare Disorders
P.O. Box 8923
New Fairfield, CT 06812
(203) 746-6518

NORD is a national nonprofit voluntary agency dedicated to the identification, control, and cure of rare disorders. Rare disorders are those affecting fewer than 200,000 Americans. NORD's programs include information and referral, education, research, service, and networking of families with the same rare disorder.

National Organization on Disability

2100 Pennsylvania Ave. N.W.
Washington, DC 20037
(800) 248-2253

NOD offers information and referral services to all handicapped individuals. The organization is community based and supports a national network of disabled people working together for change.

National Parent Network on Disabilities (NPND)

1600 Prince St., Suite #115
Alexandria, VA 22314-2836
(703) 684-6763 (Voice/TDD)

NPND is a non-profit organization dedicated to improving the lives of children, youth, and adults with disabilities and their families. Services that NPND currently provides, or will provide, include legislative representation, reference and referral, national and regional conferences, outreach to parents, materials development and distribution, and a database to link parents to local, state, regional, national and/or international services.

National Rehabilitation Association (NRA)

633 S. Washington St.
Alexandria, VA 22314
(703) 836-0850 (Voice) (703) 836-0852 (TDD)

The NRA membership is comprised of persons with disabilities, professional rehabilitation workers, and others from the fields of education, medicine, business, and industry. Members receive eight newsletters annually and the *Journal of*

Rehabilitation quarterly. NRA is active in areas such as advocacy, legislative design, and the development of education and training programs for people with disabilities. The separate professional divisions are Job Placement, Rehabilitation Counseling, Rehabilitation Administration, Vocational Evaluation and Work Adjustment, Independent Living, Rehabilitation Instructors, and Support Staff. The Association has 60 affiliate chapters throughout the country.

National Rehabilitation Information Center

8455 Colesville Rd., Suite 935
Silver Spring, MD 20910-3319
(800) 346-2742

The center provides information services to include reference services, referral services, custom searches, and subscription service. The center also has information products such as REHABDATA Thesaurus, Guide to Periodicals, NARIC Quarterly, REHAB Briefs, and Resource Guides.

National Society for Autistic Children (NSAC)

1234 Massachusetts Ave. N.W.
Washington, DC 20005
(202) 783-0125

This organization provides information relating to computers and autistic children. It is an organization for parents, teachers, psychologists, and others interested in the welfare of children with severe disorders of communication and behavior. It seeks to inform the public of the symptoms and problems of autistic children and adults.

National Special Education Alliance
Apple Computer, Inc.
20525 Mariani Ave., M/S 435
Cupertino, CA 95014
(408) 974-7910

The Alliance is a coalition of community resource centers, professional organizations, and technology vendors working together to increase the ways microcomputers can assist individuals with disabilities. Electronic linkage among centers and a national database allows information sharing about special education and rehabilitation. Training and technical assistance are available.

National Spinal Cord Injury Association
149 California St.
Newton, MA 02158
(617) 964-0521

This association provides information or referrals for the direct care of para- or quadriplegic persons. It publishes a variety of materials for rehabilitation professionals and persons with spinal cord injuries.

National Technical Institute for the Deaf (NTID)
1 Lomb Memorial Dr.
Rochester, NY 14623
(716) 475-6400

This organization of the U.S. Department of Education is a resource center on technical education for deaf and hearing-impaired people. NTID is colocated with the Rochester Institute of Technology. NTID has developed sign language training programs that can be used with computers.

New Jersey Coalition for the Advancement of Rehabilitation Technology

Bell Communications Research
Morristown, NJ 07960
(201) 829-2000

This advocacy group serves as a clearinghouse for information on public and private funding of various types of rehabilitation technology.

North Mississippi Retardation Center
P.O. Box 967
Oxford, MS 38655
(601) 234-1476

This center's research focuses on strategies for pre- and nonliterate, nonvocal, multiply handicapped persons. It developed a categorically structured pictographic display communication program for single switch users.

On-Board Solutions
103 E. Third St.
Lewes, DE 19958
(302) 645-7740

On-Board Solutions is a sales and consulting service providing supportive services to schools, rehabilitation facilities and individuals in regards to technology applied to individuals with disability. The group is an authorized dealer for many assistive devices and software for special education. The group offers free data base software searches, product information, preview opportunities and consultation.

Orton Dyslexia Society
724 York Rd.
Towson, MD 21204
(301) 296-0232, (800) 222-3123

The Orton Dyslexia Society is an international scientific and educational association concerned with the widespread problem of the specific language disability of developmental dyslexia. Local and state chapters may serve as literacy resources for dyslexic adults and those who teach or advise them.

Paralyzed Veterans of America (PVA)
801 18th St., NW
Washington, DC 20006
(202) 872-1300
   PVA is a nationwide veterans' service organization dedicated to serving the needs of America's paralyzed veterans and to representing the concerns of all veterans and members of the disability community. The national organization and its chapters throughout the United States and Puerto Rico are actively involved in spinal cord research, health, wheelchair sports/recreation programs, and general accessibility to society for physically-challenged individuals.

Parent Educational Advocacy Training Center (PEATC)
228 S. Pitt St.
Alexandria, VA 22314
(703) 836-2953, (703) 836-3026
   (TDD), (800) 869-6782 (MD, VA, and WV only)
   PEATC provides educational consultation services and conducts parent training courses in the Washington, DC metropolitan area, which are open to anyone able to attend from across the country. Participants in the three or four-day courses come in mixed pairs (i.e. parent/teacher or parent/VR counselor) and agree to return to their community and teach the curriculum just learned. Among their courses are "Next Steps: Planning for Employment," "Supported Em-

ployment Opportunities," and "World of Work." PEATC publishes a quarterly newsletter, *The PEATC Press,* which is available free of charge.

Parents Helping Parents (PHP)
535 Race St.
San Jose, CA 95126
(408) 288-5010 (Voice)
   The Center is a private non-profit organization providing: information referrals; a siblings program; professional and community networking programs; peer counseling; and support programs to families who have children with special health and educational needs. Through a grant from the U.S. Department of Health and Human Services and Maternal Child Health, it runs the *National Center for Developing Parent-to-Parent Family Resource Centers.* Manuals, booklets, and telephone or on-site consulting are available to new parent groups.

Personal Computer Opportunities for the Handicapped
P.O. Box 374
Spicer, MN 56288
(612) 796-5765
   This organization is dedicated to helping disabled individuals acquire job skills and jobs with personal computers.

President's Committee on Employment of People with Disabilities
1111 20th St., NW, Suite 636
Washington, DC 20036
(202) 653-5044, (202) 653-5050
   (TDD)
   The President's Committee is a national source of information and assistance concerning employment and people with disabilities. It can

refer callers to committees at the state and local levels. The Committee sponsors the observance of National Disability Employment Awareness Month (October), an annual conference on the employment of people with disabilities, seminars, and workshops on a range of issues concerning employment. It publishes and distributes a newsletter, *Tips and Trends,* and a quarterly magazine, *Worklife.* The Committee also sponsors the Job Accommodation Network listed above.

Project Cable
The Carroll Center for the Blind
770 Centre St.
Newton, MA 02158-2597
(617) 969-6200
   Project Cable provides computer assessment, computer training (on adaptive devices) and software, professional training, resources (on devices), and word processing for visually impaired high school students.

Project MUSE (Microcomputer Use in Special Education)
Western Illinois University
27 Horrabin Hall
Macomb, IL 61455
(309) 298-1014
   MUSE provides microcomputer training to special education teachers for a fee. Participants are trained to teach others what they have learned.

PSI-TECH
Concepts for Independent Living
2203 Airport Way South
Seattle, WA 98134
(206) 343-0670
   The PSI-TECH program serves the needs of individuals with disability through three interrelated elements: TECH-NET; TECH Teams; and Research Council.

Recording for the Blind, Inc.
20 Roszel Rd.
Trenton, NJ 08540
(609) 452-0606
   Recording for the Blind, Inc. records educational books for persons with visual, physical, or specific learning disabilities who meet eligibility guidelines.

Registry of Interpreters for the Deaf (RID)
8719 Colesville Rd.
Suite #310
Silver Spring, MD 20910
(301) 608-0050 (Voice/TDD)
   RID is a membership organization with almost 4,000 members, who include professional interpreters and transliterators, interpreter/transliterator educators, students, persons with deafness or hearing impairment and professionals in related fields. The purpose of RID is to initiate, sponsor, promote, and execute policies and activities that will further the profession of interpretation of American Sign Language and the transliteration of English. RID has 57 affiliate chapters in the United States and Canada.

Rehabilitation Engineering Center
Children's Hospital at Stanford
520 Sand Hill Rd.
Palo Alto, CA 94304
(415) 327-4800 × 345
   This center provides evaluations to determine computer access, appropriate hardware, software, and work station setup. It provides augmentative communication systems and seating systems for optimum positioning.

Rehabilitation Information Service
Maryland Department of Health
  and Mental Hygiene
Office of Chronic and Rehabilitation
  Facilities
Baltimore, MD 21201
(800) 638-8864
  The Rehabilitation Information
Service is operated by the Maryland
Department of Health and Mental
Hygiene as a service to people who
have had a spinal cord injury, a
stroke, an amputation, a head in-
jury, or other physical disability.

Rehabilitation Institute of Ohio
Miami Valley Hospital
Dayton, OH 45409
(513) 220-2063
  The Institute uses computers to
help brain injured individuals make
maximum use of their abilities.
Focus is on cognitive and linguistic
retraining using microcomputers as
therapeutic tools.

Rehabilitation International (RI)
25 E. 21st St.
New York, NY 10018
(212) 420-1500
  RI is a federation of 135 organizations in 81 countries conducting programs to assist people with disabilities and all who work for prevention,
rehabilitation, and integration. It
publishes the International Rehabilitation Review to report on worldwide scientific developments in the
fields of disability, rehabilitation,
and related fields.

Rehabilitation Research Center
Wright and Filippis, Inc.
Rochester Hills, MI 48063
(313) 853-1830
  The Rehabilitation Research Cen-
ter is a nonprofit facility for re-

search, education, and training in
rehabilitation methods, techniques,
and systems for the physically and
mentally impaired.

Rehabilitation Technology Center
South Bend Memorial Hospital
6535 E. 82nd St.
Indianapolis, IN 46250
(317) 845-3408
  This center provides services in
augmentative/alternative communication, seating/positioning, mobility,
environmental control, computer access, and home/job site modifications.

Rehabilitation Technology Center
  of Pittsburgh
Rehabilitation Institute of Pittsburgh
Rehabilitation Technology Center
Pittsburgh, PA 15217
(412) 521-9000
  The Rehabilitation Technology
Center is a vendor of high-technol-
ogy assistive devices for individuals
who have physical limitations. These
devices address the needs of persons
who may require augmentative/
alternative communication; environmental control; computer access
and/or wheelchair mobility.

Rehabotics, Inc.
P.O. Box 10751
Portland, OR 97210-0751
(503) 297-5061
  Specializing in robotic and computer workstations for the work,
education, and home environment.

The Research and Training Center
  on Independent Living (RTC/IL)
University of Kansas
BCR 3111 Haworth
Lawrence, KS 66045
(913) 864-4095 (Voice/TDD)

The Research and Training Center on Independent Living was established in 1980 under a grant from NIDRR. Its mission is to develop, test, and disseminate materials to over 350 independent living centers (ILCs) nationwide, who serve consumers with various types of disabilities. RTC/IL research-tested materials are developed with extensive input from consumers with disabilities. The center has training materials and workshops in Personal and Systems Advocacy; ILC Evaluation; Consumer Management of Personal Assistants; Self-Help Group Leader Training; Positive Media Portrayal of Persons with Disabilities; Mentoring; Developing Slike Presentations to Promote Community Support; and other material related to independent living. The RTC/IL conducts an annual national Independent Living Conference for ILCs and people with disabilities, and publishes a quarterly newsletter, *The Independent Living Forum*. A complete bibliography of materials is available free upon request.

RESNA
Suite 700
Washington, DC 20036
(202) 857-1199

RESNA, an interdisciplinary association for the advancement of rehabilitation and assistive technology, is concerned with transferring science, engineering, and technology information to the needs of persons with disabilities. Its members are rehabilitation professionals from all pertinent disciplines, providers, and consumers. The goal is to promote interaction among these groups to better understand and serve the needs of those who can benefit from rehabilitation technology.

Resource Center
Colorado Easter Seal Society, Inc.
609 W. Littleton Blvd.
Littleton, CO 80120
(303) 795-2016

This center offers a variety of computer services for disabled people, including computer camps; workshops for disabled individuals, teachers, and therapists, and information on computers and adaptive equipment.

Resources for Rehabilitation
33 Bradford St., Suite 19A
Lexington, MA 02173
(617) 862-6455

Resources for Rehabilitation is a non-profit organization that produces the *"Living with Low Vision"* series of publications. Professional publications include *Rehabilitation Resource Manual: VISION* ($39.95 plus $4.50 shipping/handling) and *Providing Services for People with Vision Loss: A Multidisciplinary Perspective* ($19.95 plus $3 shipping/handling). *Living with Low Vision: A Resource Guide for People with Sight Loss* ($35 plus shipping/handling) is a large print directory that enables people with visual impairments to find the assistance they need to remain independent. A special series of large print publications designed for distribution by professionals to people with vision loss includes *Living with Low Vision, Living with Diabetic Retinopathy, Children and Adolescents with Vision Loss, High Tech Aids for People with Vision Loss,* and *Aids for Everyday Living with Vision Loss.* Resources for Rehabilitation also conducts training programs on vision loss and will custom design a program to meet an organization's special needs.

Rocky Mountain Regional Center for Augmentative Communication
Boulder Memorial Hospital
311 Mapleton
Boulder, CO 80302
(303) 441-0461
The Center has a variety of electronic and nonelectronic aids used to assess client's augmentative communication needs. Professionals design ways to strengthen communication abilities.

SEDL/Regional Rehabilitation Exchange
211 E. 7th St.
Austin, TX 78701
(512) 476-6861
This project identifies exemplary practices and programs. The core area is "High Technology Applications in the Vocational Rehabilitation Process." Technical assistance in this area is provided.

Selective Systems for Living
2500 Riverside Ave.
Minneapolis, MN 55454
(612) 375-0153
This group provides workshops on special input devices, environmental control devices, and word processing. It also assists clients in procuring computer systems. The goal is to link handicapped people to computers and employment.

Self-Help for Hard of Hearing People, Inc. (SHHH)
7800 Wisconsin Ave.
Bethesda, MD 20814
(301) 657-2248, (301) 657-2249 (TDD)

SHHH is a volunteer, international organization of hard of hearing people, their relatives and friends. It is a non-profit, nonsectarian educational organization devoted to the welfare and interests of those with partial hearing who are committed to participating in the hearing world.

Sensory Assistance Center
Department of Justice
Washington, DC 20530
(202) 633-5104
This organization is a service and training center for blind and vision-impaired federal employees. Services include training in the use of computers and demonstrations of new and existing devices.

SETUP
Special Education Technology Users Project
3430 Leahi Ave.
Honolulu, HI 96815
(808) 737-2377
SETUP is a federally funded project that trains special education teachers in the state of Hawaii to utilize the computer as a tool for computer managed instruction and computer assisted instruction.

70001, Training and Employment, Ltd.
501 School St., SW, Suite 600
Washington, DC 20024
(202) 484-0103
70001 is a national nonprofit organization operating local programs for at-risk youth in DC between 18 and 21 years of age and many cities across the country, including Drop-Out Recovery Programs and Drop-Out Prevention Programs. Call or write to obtain a referral to a local

group, or to receive their free bi-monthly newsletter, *Going Places*.

Sibling Information Network
991 Main St., Suite 3A
East Hartford, CT 06108
(203) 282-7050
The Network was established to assist individuals interested in the needs of families of persons with disabilities. It offers a state-by-state listing of sibling support groups. A newsletter, *Sibling Information Network News,* is published four times a year to describe projects, literature, research findings, and ideas useful to siblings of a person with a disability. Membership in the Network is $7/year for individuals and $15/year for organizations.

Sister Kenny Institute
Division of Abbot-Northwestern
  Hospital
800 E. 28th St. at Chicago Ave.
Minneapolis, MN 55407
(612) 874-4175
This organization uses computer programs to provide language and cognitive therapy to adults with neurologic injuries.

Smart Exchange
P.O. Box 675165
Marietta, GA 30067-0011
(404) 988-1180
The Smart Exchange is a network that offers service providers within the states of: Alabama, Florida, Georgia, Kentucky, North Carolina, South Carolina and Tennessee an opportunity to showcase their programs as well as assist in the replication of innovative methods and applications proven successful. The Smart Exchange is seeking to identify exemplary programs in effective

rehabilitation technology in the following programs: early intervention, education, transitional services, employment, independent living and recreation and leisure.

Social Security Administration
U.S. Department of Health and
  Human Services
Local Telephone Directory: U.S.
  Government Section (Blue Pages)
(800) 234-5772, (800) 325-0778
  (TDD)
Local offices of SSA across the country have pamphlets about benefits relating to disability. Staff can answer questions relating to SSI and SSDI over the phone, as well as in writing.

Software Evaluation Clearing-
  house for Educators of the
  Hearing Impaired
Learning Resources Center
Model Secondary School for the
  Deaf
Washington, DC 20002
(202) 651-5333
This center serves as an evaluation information clearinghouse and lending library of microcomputer software for schools and programs involved with the education of hearing impaired students.

Solutions Through Technology for
  People with Disabilities
DeWitt, Mendelsohn & Associates
62 Oak Knoll Rd.
Glen Rock, NJ 07452-1632
(201) 447-5585
Solutions Through Technology for People with Disabilities is a project of a consulting group working in four major areas: public policy analysis, retention strategies, market re-

search and strategic planning and human factors guidance for companies in the design of universally accessible products and services.

Special Education Software-Hardware Review Center
Teacher Center
232 Churchwell Ave.
Knoxville, TN 37917
(615) 544-4450
This center consolidates information on products used in special education. The center serves private and public institutions serving the disabled individual.

Special Education Technology Resource Center
Emmanuel College Library
Boston, MA 02115
(617) 232-7913
The Center maintains a software lending library, model adaptive hardware learning lab, and a variety of teacher training opportunities for Special Educators.

Specialized Training of Military Parents (STOMP)
12208 Pacific Hwy., SE
Tacoma, WA 98499
(206) 588-1741

1851 Ram Runway, Suite 102
College Park, GA 30337
(404) 761-2745
The STOMP Project provides individual assistance to families; workshops; assistance and site visits to other Parent Training and Information (PTI centers; and national workshops for Military Parent Leaders. Topics of expertise include P.L. 94-142, P.L. 99457, Section 504, overseas schools, Section VI schools), CHAMPUS, and discrimi-

nation regulations for Armed Services. STOMP can go into military bases and work with hospitals, commanders, Exceptional Family Member Programs (EFMP), and other service providers. Families can call the project collect for assistance.

Spina Bifida Association of America
343 S. Dearborn St., Suite 310
Chicago, IL 60604
(312) 663-1562
Spina Bifida is a network of chapters dedicated to increasing awareness of the problems and potentials of individuals born with Spina Bifida. The Association believes all persons, disabled and nondisabled, are entitled to the same fundamental human rights.

Spinal Cord Injury Hotline
American Paralysis Association (APA)
c/o Montebello Rehabilitation Hospital
2201 Argonne Dr.
Baltimore, MD 21218
(800) 526-3456
The Spinal Cord Injury Hotline is a toll-free information and referral service. It is available to individuals who have sustained a spinal cord injury and to their families. It facilitates the search for support and resources by referring callers to individuals having personal experience with spinal cord injury (peer contacts), or to professionals or organizations with expertise in these areas. The Hotline works with individuals to solve a wide range of problems and to direct them to the most current and helpful resources.

Storer Computer Access Center
Cleveland Society for the Blind
1909 E. 101st St.
Cleveland, OH 44106
(216) 791-8118

The Storer Computer Access
Center provides services over the
telephone, on-site, or at the Center.
Services provided include orientation to available alternative access
systems, evaluation of prerequisite
skills, applications-oriented system
assessment, training on hardware
and software, technical consultation
and engineering support, and in-
service training for educators,
counselors, and instructors.

**Support Program for Handicapped
Federal Employees**
Government Services Administration
Support Programs for the Handi-
capped
Washington, DC
(202) 523-1906

The Support Program for Handicapped Federal Employees is operated by the Government Services
Administration (GSA). The program
provides technical support for assistive computer equipment and access
technology. The program is also involved in disseminating information
on Section 508.

**TAM (Technology & Media
Division)**
Council for Exceptional Children
1920 Association Dr.
Reston, VA 22091-1589
(703) 620-3660, (703) 264-9463,
(800) 873-8255

This division of the Council for
Exceptional Children keeps abreast
of the latest technological advances
in Special Education, provides training, and publishes a monthly newsletter.

TASH
The Association for Persons with
Severe Handicaps
7010 Roosevelt Way N.E.
Seattle, WA 98115
(206) 523-8446

TASH offers information on se-
vere-profound handicaps (particularly
severe retardation). It maintains an
extensive bookstore of books and
papers regarding persons with severe
handicaps. Manufacturer of assistive
devices.

**Technical Assistance for Parent
Programs (TAPP)**
Federation for Children with Special
Needs
312 Stuart St.
Boston, MA 02116
(617) 482-2915

The TAPP Network is federally
funded with Special Needs and the
U.S. Department of Education to
provide training to parent groups
through four regional centers. It is a
project of the National Network of
Parent Centers described above.
TAPP publishes *Coalition Quarterly;* it
has a list of monographs; and it conducts national and regional conferences. The Regional Centers will
refer callers to the closest parent
group. They can provide information about parenting youth in transition, either from school to work or
from school to further education and
training. Northeast Regional
Center, Parent Information Center,
P.O. Box 1422, Concord, NH
03302, (603) 224-7005; Midwest
Regional Center, PACER Center,
4826 Chicago Ave., South, Minneapolis, MN 55417, (612) 827-2966;
South Regional Center, PEP,
Georgia ARC, 1851 Ram Runway,
#104, College Park, GA 30337,

(404) 761-3150; West Regional
Center, Washington State PAVE,
6316 S. 12th St., Tacoma, WA
98465, (206) 565-2266.

**Technical Assistance for Special
  Populations Program (TASPP)**
National Center for Research in
  Vocational Education (NCRVE)
University of Illinois Site
345 Education Bldg.
1310 S. Sixth St.
Champaign, IL 61820
(217) 333-0807
   TASPP, a service function of the
National Center for Research in
Vocational Education, University of
California, Berkeley, is housed at
the University of Illinois. TASPP is
designed to assist in the improvement of vocational education programs for youth and adults with
special needs. TASPP produces
materials, responds to inquiries
about vocational programs for special groups, and provides an array
of services for professionals serving
special populations in vocational
education. Publications include the
TASPP BULLETIN, a quarterly
newsletter on critical issues and
policy options; *TASPP BRIEF,* a
topical paper highlighting the
latest research, the newest resources,
and exemplary programs for each
theme explored by TASPP; and
resource guides (available at cost
recovery prices) on transition, youth
at risk, teen parents, persons with
limited English, and both rural and
urban resources in vocational education. The *BULLETIN, BRIEF,*
and TASPP computerized information searches are available
at no charge. The list of NCRVE
publications is available upon request.

Technical Resource Centre
1820 Richmond Rd. S.W.
Calgary, AB T2T 5C7
(403) 229-7875
   TRC provides information and a
one-month loan of devices in the
areas of adaptive toys, communication, aids to daily living, inventory
control, and microcomputers. The
Center offers assessment and consultation.

Technology Access Alliance
Personal Computer Resources, Inc.
2100 Washington St.
Hanover, MA 02339
(617) 871-5396
   The purpose of the Technology
Access Alliance (TAA) is to further
the understanding of how technology can increase independence for
persons of all ages who are physically, mentally and emotionally challenged. TAA will also facilitate the
distribution of assistive technology
and provide training on how to use
assistive technology products.

**Technology Center for Special
  Education**
University of Missouri — Kansas City
School of Education, Rm. 24
Kansas City, MO
64110-2499
(816) 276-1040
   The Technology Center for Special Education provides information
and technical assistance, specialized
training, and access to a cataloged
collection of software and hardware
computer information.

**Technology for Language and
  Learning**
P.O. Box 327
East Rockaway, NY 11518-0327
No phone

Technology for Language and Learning is a nonprofit organization dedicated to advancing the use of technology and computers with children and adults with special needs. One of the activities is to create and collect high-quality public-domain software. These programs are then distributed to parents, educators and organizations involved with children or adults with language impairments or learning and physical disabilities.

Technology-Related Assistance for Individuals with Disabilities
National Institute on Disability
   and Rehabilitation Research
   (NIDRR)
Switzer Bldg.
400 Maryland Ave., SW
Washington, DC 20202
(202) 732-5066

The Technology-Related Assistance for Individuals with Disabilities Act of 1988 was signed into law on August 19, 1988. The purpose of the Act is to assist each state in developing and implementing a consumer-responsive statewide program of technology-related assistance for individuals of all ages with disabilities. Assistive technology are powerful tools that can provide the necessary means for individuals with disabilities to have greater control over their lives; participate more actively in school, at work, and community; interact to a greater extent with peers; and to become more independent. In FY 1989, nine states were funded. Those states are: Arkansas, Colorado, Illinois, Kentucky, Maine, Maryland, Minnesota, Nebraska, and Utah. RESNA was awarded the technical assistance contract. In FY 1990, an additional 13 states received funding. Those

states are: Alaska, Indiana, Iowa, Massachusetts, Mississippi, Nevada, New Mexico, North Carolina, Oregon, Tennessee, Vermont, Virginia, and Wisconsin.

Telecommunications for the Deaf, Inc. (TDI)
814 Thayer Ave.
Silver Spring, MD 20910
(301) 589-3006 (Voice/TDD)

TDI addresses issues related to telecommunications for the deaf. In addition to publishing an annual national directory of TDD numbers, it is a non-profit membership organization providing information and assistance on telecommunication issues. The annual directory is $12.50. Membership fees are $15 for an individual and $30 for an organization. The quarterly newsletter, GA-SK, covers information about telecommunications. TDI offers to be a link between a consumer who is developing a visual communication device and a manufacturer willing to produce it.

Thresholds Psychiatric Rehabilitation Center
2700 Lakeview Ave.
Chicago, IL 60614
(312) 281-3800

Thresholds is a psychosocial rehabilitation agency serving persons with severe and persistent mental illness. It promotes improved service and functioning in six areas: vocation, independent living, education, social skills, avoidance of rehospitalization, and physical health. Grants from the U.S. Office of Education support the *Supported Competitive Employment Newsletter;* a manual for parents called *Strengthening Skills for Success: A Manual to Help Parents Sup-*

port their *Psychiatrically Disabled Youth's Community Employment;* and the *Community Exploration Program,* a curriculum to encourage withdrawn people to go out, to be aware of employment opportunities, and to use appropriate skills in those settings. Specifically related to postsecondary education are: *Addressing Problems with Postsecondary Vocational Education and Guide to Choosing a Postsecondary School for Psychiatrically Disabled Youth.*

Trace Research and Development Center
Trace Center
S-151 Waisman Center
Madison, WI 53705
(608) 262-6966
This nationally recognized organization develops and disseminates information related to nonvocal communication, computer access, and technology for handicapped persons.

Travelin' Talk
P.O. Box 3534
Clarksville, TN 37043-3534
(615) 552-6670, FAX: (615) 552-1182
Travelin' Talk is an international network of people providing assistance to travelers with disabilities by sharing their knowledge and/or extending services travelers may need while visiting, passing through, or planning their trips. Quarterly newsletter, *Travelin' Talk* is available to share resources, tips and stories of ways people are helping each other.

Typewriting Institute for the Handicapped
3102 W. Augusta Ave.
Phoenix, AZ 85051
(602) 939-5344

The Institute is a for-profit company which makes the Dvorak one-hand keyboard for typewriters and word processors that are rearranged to accommodate one-handed typing. Other products to promote independence listed in the catalogue include two sizes of large print typewriters for people with low vision and "end 0 line light" for the deaf typist.

United Cerebral Palsy Associations
66 E. 34th St.
New York, NY 10016
(212) 481-6300, (800) 872-1827

UCP Community Services Division
1522 K St., NW, Suite 1112
Washington, DC 20005
(202) 842-1266
UCP is a nationwide direct service organization with over 225 affiliates, each of which provides its own array of services ranging from pre-school to adult work programs. UCP sponsors research and advocacy, as well as publishing pamphlets, articles, film/slide presentations, and display materials. Some are free; others are available for a small fee, and several are in Spanish as well as English. A quarterly magazine, *UCP News,* is available by request to the New York address. The monthly *Word from Washington,* which tracks legislation that impacts disabled people, is available from the UCP Community Services Division. (Parents of persons with disabilities $25/year; all others, $55/year).

United States Society for Augmentative and Alternative Communication
c/o Barkley Memorial Center
Lincoln, NE 68588
(402) 472-5463

USSAAC is a national chapter of
the International Society for Augmentative and Alternative Communication. The goals of USSACC
are to enhance the communication
effectiveness of persons who can
benefit from augmentative and alternative communication.

**Voice Indexing for the Blind, Inc.
  (VIB)**
7420 Westlake Terrace #203
Bethesda, MD 20817
(301) 469-9470
VIB instructs in voice indexing,
which enables users to highlight and
scan taped material. It also produces
voice-indexed recordings on contract, and lectures on how print-
handicapped persons can access
reference materials. *Procedure for Sequential Voice-Indexing on a 2-Track or
4-Track Cassette Recorder* and *Voice-
Indexed Cassettes* (a catalogue) are
available in large print and on
voice-indexed cassettes. Note that
voice indexing is a helpful skill for
students with writing difficulty and
learning disabilities as well as vision
impairments.

Washington Apple Pi
8227 Woodmont Ave.
Bethesda, MD 20814
(301) 654-8060
This organization of Apple Computer users meet and discuss all
aspects of Apple Computers. Many
of the topics are applicable to disabled individuals. The organization
publishes Washington Apple Pi
Journal.

**Western New York Resource
  Center for Applied Technology**
UCPA of WNY, Inc.
7 Community Dr.

Buffalo, NY 14225
(716) 894-1432
The WNY Resource Center for
Applied Technology provides technological assistance for client-
oriented computer applications for
persons with special needs. Support
is available for special education
teachers, therapists, rehabilitation
specialists, and all professionals with
an interest in the utilization of computer technology to enhance the
abilities of the disabled person.

Woods Sensory Assistance Center
United States Department of Justice
Washington, DC 20510
(202) 633-5104
The Woods Sensory Assistance
Center is operated by the United
States Department of Justice. It is a
demonstration and training center
for computer access technology for
visually impaired employees of the
Department of Justice and other
Federal agencies.

**World Institute on Disability
  (WID)**
510 16th St.
Oakland, CA 94612
(415) 763-4100 (Voice/TDD)
WID is a public policy institute
seeking solutions to major problems
faced by disabled people of all ages.
Founded in 1983, it offers information on independent living, personal
attendant care, and study results of
the IDEAS project in foreign countries.

**Worldwide Disability Solutions
  Group**
Apple Computer, Inc.
20525 Mariani Ave., MS 2SE
Cupertino, CA 95014
(408) 974-7910, (408) 974-7911 (TDD)

Through this office, Apple works with key education, rehabilitation, and advocacy organizations nationwide to identify the computer-related needs of disabled individuals and to assist in the development of responsive programs. The Worldwide Disability Solutions Group is also involved in insuring Apple computers are accessible. The office is the founding corporate sponsor of the Alliance for Technology Access (ATA).

Yankton Area Adjustment Training Center
909 W. 23rd St.
Yankton, SD 57078
(605) 665-2518

The Center provides computer assisted learning on the Apple IIe for area special education students. Focus includes job skills, job readiness skills, math skills, time and money skills, pedestrian safety, and motivation.

Young Adult Institute (YAI)
460 W. 34th St.
New York, NY 10001
(212) 563-7474

YAI is a non-profit professional organization serving developmentally disabled children and adults in many programs throughout the New York metropolitan area. Available on a national basis are: videotapes, manuals, and guides for training parents and professionals, including the widely acclaimed videos *On Our Own* and *Children with Special Needs*. YAI holds an annual international conference. A recent addition to training materials focused on young adults with developmental disabilities and AIDS. Some services and materials are free of charge, and a catalogue is available.

Appendix E: Publications

Accent on Living
Accent on Information
Box 700
Bloomington, IL 61701
(309) 378-2961

This magazine contains articles of general interest for physically disabled individuals, their families, and professionals and lay persons who work with them.

ACCESS
Project Access
Special Education Services
Lansing, MI 48909
(800) 922-2377

This newsletter is published by Project Access of the Wayne County School District in Wayne, Michigan. The newsletter addresses the computer concerns of educators of special students. The newsletter contains information on conferences, new products and general computer related news.

ACTT Outreach
Activating Children Through Technology (ACTT)
Project ACTT
Macomb, IL 61455
(309) 298-1634

This newsletter updates the ser-

vices provided by ACTT (Activating Children Through Technology).

ACTT provides training to teachers to integrate computer technology into their programs for children who are disabled.

ACTT has also developed products and curriculum for use with young handicapped children.

Add-Ons: The Ultimate Guide to Peripherals for the Blind Computer User
National Braille Press
88 St. Stephen St.
Boston, MA 02115
(617) 266-6160

1986. 259 pages. $19.95. Braille and cassette editions, $16.95.

(The) Advocate
National Society for Autistic Children
1234 Massachusetts Ave. N.W.
Washington, DC 20005
(202) 783-0125

Advocate contains current information relating microcomputers to the teaching of autistic children. It also lists information concerning conferences relating to computers and autism.

Aids and Appliances Review
The Carroll Center for the Blind

770 Centre St.
Newton, MA 02158-2597
(617) 969-6200

Aids and Appliances Review offers reviews of products available for blind or vision impaired individuals. It contains articles for professionals and lay persons concerned about blind and vision impaired individuals.

Alert

Association of Handicapped Student Service Programs in Postsecondary Education
P.O. Box 21192
Columbus, OH 43221
(614) 488-4972

Alert is published 6 times per year by the Association of Handicapped Student Service Programs in Postsecondary Education. It contains information of interest to disabled postsecondary students.

ALS Association Newsletter

Amyotrophic Lateral Sclerosis Society (ALS)
15300 Ventura Blvd., Suite 315
Sherman Oaks, CA 91403
(213) 990-2151

This newsletter contains summaries of available computer-assisted communication appliances and devices. New developments in the computer-assisted communication field are covered in each issue.

American Foundation for the Blind's Publications Catalog

American Foundation for the Blind, Inc.
15 W. 16th St.
New York, NY 10011
(800) 232-5463

This catalog is available in print and on cassette. It lists 95 textbooks,

periodicals, guides, manuals, research papers, and general information publications that are of interest to blind and visually impaired people. Many of the publications are available in large-print, braille, and on cassette.

American Journal of Occupational Therapy

American Occupational Therapy Association
1383 Piccard Dr.
Rockville, MD 20850
(301) 948-9626

This professional journal lists new approaches, practices, research, educational activities, and trends in occupational therapy.

Apple Computer Resources in Special Education and Rehabilitation

DLM Teaching Resources
One DLM Park
Allen, TX 75002
(800) 527-4747, (800) 442-4711

Developed by Apple Office of Special Education in conjunction with Trace Center and Closing the Gap. 1989. $19.95. This book combines the 1987 book and the 1989 update information. If you purchased the 1987 version and filled in one of the cards attached to the back cover, you have received the update information free, and don't need this new book.

Apple Talk

3015 S. Tyler St.
Little Rock, AR 72204
(501) 666-6552

A quarterly magazine for blind and visually impaired individuals, this is available on computer disks and includes articles about program ming, notices about computer products and software, games, and utility programs.

Assistive Device News
Pennsylvania Assistive Device
    Center
150 S. Progress Ave.
Harrisburg, PA 17109
(800) 222-7372
    The *Assistive Device News* is published by the Pennsylvania Assistive Device Center located at the Elizabethtown Hospital and Rehabilitation Center. It is published as a service to the Central Pennsylvania Special Education Regional Resource Center.

Assistive Technology Design in
    Special Education
Council for Exceptional Children
1920 Association Dr.
Reston, VA 22091-1589
(703) 620-3660, (703) 264-9463,
    (800) 873-8255
    This document contains information on the principles, issues and design features discovered or used by the Office of Special Education Programs (OSEP) projects funded to date (1990) and illustrates these principles with examples from the projects themselves. The information is presented according to three major stages in assistive technology development: designing to fit user needs; prototype development, testing and evaluation and distribution.

Augmentative and Alternative
    Communication Journal
Williams and Wilkins
428 E. Preston St.
Baltimore, MD 21202
(800) 638-6423
    This professional journal focuses

on nonverbal communication, integration theory, technology, systems development, assessment, treatment, and education of users who rely on augmentative or assistive communication systems.

Augmentative Communication:
    Implementation Strategies
American Speech-Language-Hearing
    Association
10801 Rockville Pike
Rockville, MD 20852
(301) 897-5700
    Augmentative Communication: Implementation Strategies is a book that offers techniques for introducing, managing and evaluating augmentative communication programs in schools, clinics, hospitals and nursing homes. Chapters tell how to identify and evaluate users; acquire, distribute and maintain equipment and materials; encourage community and caregiver participation; conduct professional staff development; and initiate and improve program administration.

Augmentative Communication
    News
Sunset Enterprises
One Surf Way
Monterey, CA 93940
(408) 649-3050
    Augmentative Communication News is a newsletter dedicated to the field of assistive and augmentative communication. Sections of the newsletter deal with information of interest to consumers and clinicians. Sections of the newsletter are also dedicated to equipment, research, and government.

BAUD
MicroTalk

Publishing Division
337 South Peterson Ave.
Louisville, KY 40206
(502) 896-1288
Bimonthly; $24/year cassette tape; $30/yr diskette. Networking newsletter reports on subjects of interest to blind and visually impaired Apple computer users. Editor runs an exchange program for public domain software.

BITS and PIECES
Massachusett's Rehabilitation Commission Library
22th Fl., Statler Office Bldg.
Boston, MA 02116
(617) 727-1140
This is a bimonthly newsletter and acquisitions list of the Massachusetts Rehabilitation and Commission Library. The Library has a large collection of disability and rehabilitation information.

Braille Book Review and Talking Book Topics
Library of Congress
Washington, DC 20542
(800) 424-9100
Braille Book Review contains descriptions of books newly printed in braille and a list of braille magazines. *Talking Book Topics* is published bimonthly and distributed free to blind and physically impaired individuals.

Bulletin of Science and Technology for the Handicapped
American Association for the Advancement of Science
1776 Massachusetts Ave. NW
Washington, DC 20036
(202) 467-4496
The *Bulletin* includes articles on technology and its users. These ar-

ticles contain summaries of current research on technology used to aid disabled individuals.

CABLEgram
Carroll Center for the Blind
770 Centre St.
Newton, MA 02158
(617) 332-9054
Quarterly, regular print, $15/year. Newsletter answers questions from blind and visually impaired users regarding computer access and applications.

Capturing the Potential: Technology Applications for Special Educators in Highe
University of Missouri—Kansas City
School of Education, Rm. 24
Kansas City, MO 64110-2499
(816) 276-1040
This publication was written as part of the ongoing efforts of the Missouri Technology Center for Special Education to provide special educators with pertinent information regarding technology and its application for students in special education. The Missouri Technology Center for Special Education, located in the School of Education at the University of Missouri—Kansas City, is a state wide technology support project funded by the Department of Elementary and Secondary Education, Division of Special Education.

Careers and the Handicapped
Equal Opportunity Publications, Inc.
44 Broadway
Greenlawn, NY 11740
(516) 261-8899
Careers and the Handicapped is a magazine dedicated to promoting

the personal and professional growth of the physically challenged.

(The) Catalyst
Western Center for Microcomputers in Special Education
1259 El Camino Real, Suite 275
Menlo Park, CA 94025
(415) 326-6997
This quarterly newsletter publishes updated information, essays, and helpful hints on the use of microcomputers in special education.

CHIME Newsletter
Clearinghouse of Information on
   Microcomputers in Education
College of Education
Stillwater, OK 74078
(405) 624-6254
This newsletter contains teacher reviews of educational software including special education software. It offers incentives to teachers to submit reviews. All reviews are presented in a standardized format with details as to population abilities, age, grade, and subject area.

Classroom Computer Learning
Peter Li, Inc.
2169 Francisco Blvd. East
Suite A4
San Rafael, CA 94901
(415) 457-4333
This publication contains articles and information on the use of computer technology in the classroom. It contains product reviews and suggestions for classroom teachers.

Closing the Gap
Closing the Gap, Inc.
P.O. Box 68
Henderson, MN 56044
(612) 248-3294
A widely read, bimonthly news-

paper devoted exclusively to the use of microcomputers in special education and rehabilitation, it contains software and hardware reviews, new trends, and current product and application information.

Cognitive Rehabilitation
6555 Carrollton Ave.
Indianapolis, IN 46220
(317) 257-9672
This journal includes articles on the use of computers in cognitive retraining, software reviews, and printed source code to allow readers to program new applications.

Colleges That Enable
Park Avenue Press
401 Park Ave.
Oil City, PN 16301
(814) 876-5777
This book provides a guide to support services offered to physically disabled students on 40 US campuses. The schools act as liaisons with outside agencies in the community that provide personal care and help the disabled student with any problems related to the care needs.

Communi-Collegist
Callier Center for Communication
   Disorders
1966 Inwood Rd.
Dallas, TX 75225
(214) 783-3000
This provides current information on augmentative and assistive communication materials, equipment, and literature.

Communicating Together
Easter Seal Communication Institute
250 Ferrand Dr., Suite 200
Don Mills, ON M3C 3P2
(416) 421-8377 × 2313

This quarterly journal is published by the Blissymbolics Communication Institute and covers the use of Blissymbolics with all types of communication disorders.

Communication Outlook
Artificial Language Laboratory
Michigan State University
East Lansing, MI 48824-1042
(517) 353-5399
This forum is for individuals interested in the application of techniques and aids for people who experience communication disabilities due to neurological or neuromuscular conditions.

The Communicator
Wenrich, John
Rt. 4
Hillsville, VA 24343
(703) 766-3869
This publication (available in large and regular print as well as on audio tape) pertains to technology for visually impaired individuals.

Community Colleges and Students with Disabilities — A Directory of Services/Programs
HEATH Resource Center
1 Dupont Circle
Washington, DC 20036-1193
(202) 939-9320
This publication was a joint effort of the American Association of Community and Junior Colleges and the American Council on Education. The directory is based on a Spring 1987 survey. The directory provides evidence of the role community colleges play in the education and training of students with disabilities. The directory allows users to identify programs, contact people and services at the nation's two-year colleges.

Community News
Community Service for Autistic
    Adults and Children, Inc.
751 Twinbrook Pkwy.
Rockville, MD 20851
No phone
This publication is dedicated to the proposition that all people with autism can live and have the right to be served in the community, that they have a right to fully integrated services, that all such services must be individualized, positive, specialized, and consistent with their needs and preferences.

COMPOSE
Computer Opportunities in Special
    Education
Woonsocket High School
Woonsocket, RI 02895
No phone
This newsletter is published to share information on how computers are being used in an occupational education program at a senior high school. The publisher of the newsletter hopes to develop a network of people interested in sharing information on the use of computers in special education classrooms.

ComputeAble News
ComputeAble Network
P.O. Box 1706
Portland, OR 97207
(503) 644-2940
ComputeAble News is the official magazine of the ComputeAble Network, Inc. *ComputeAble News* is a magazine for persons who have a disability. The magazine contains articles of general interest.

Computer Access in Higher Education for Students with Disabilities
High-Tech Center for the Disabled

1109 Ninth St.
Sacramento, CA 95814
(916) 322-4636

Computer Access in Higher Education for Students with Disabilities is a book that contains information about access technologies. It also contains a section dealing with the computer access needs of the severely disabled. A product guide is included that contains access programs and devices plus a curriculum guide to development of courses in adapted computer technology. The book also contains the complete text of Section 508.

Computer Application in Health Care
Haworth Press
10 Alice St.
Binghamton, NY 13904
(800) 342-9678

Fall 1986 issue (Vol. 3, Nos. 3/4) of *Occupational Therapy in Health Care,* F. Cromwell, editor.

Computer Assistance for People with Disabilities
DeskTop Marketing
100 VanNess Ave.
19th Fl.
San Francisco, CA

Neil Scott. 1987. $24.95 + $4 postage and handling.

Computer-Based Technology for Individuals with Physical Disabilities
Hugh MacMillan Medical Centre
350 Rumsey Rd.
Toronto, ON M4G 1R8
(416) 425-6220

Computer-Based Technology for Individuals with Physical Disabilities outlines guidelines to assist developers in the design of future alternate access systems for computer-based technology.

Computer Classroom News
Intentional Educations, Inc.
51 Spring St.
Watertown, MA 02172
(617) 923-7707

This magazine emphasizes the application of microcomputers in the classroom. It contains articles of general interest concerning the use of microcomputers in the classroom.

Computer-Disability News
National Easter Seal Society
70 E. Lake St.
Chicago, IL 60601
(312) 726-6200

This periodical focuses on microcomputer use with and by all disabled people. The periodical also contains articles of general interest concerning the use of microcomputers.

Computer Equipment and Aids for the Blind and Visually Impaired
Computer Center for the Visually Impaired
Baruch College
New York, NY 10010
(212) 725-3000

This publication is the result of an eight-year effort in educating blind and visually impaired individuals in computer technology. The book contains lists of suppliers of equipment, both hardware and software, suppliers of peripherals, researchers, training and demonstration centers, and products in the process of development. The publication contains indexes by product and by vendor, a glossary that makes data understandable to non-technical readers, and a "Before You Buy" section that offers a checklist of technical considerations and advice on how to select equipment appropriate for specific needs.

Computer Science Update
NFB in Computer Science
3530 N. Dupont
Minneapolis, MN 55410
  Semi-annual, regular print, $2.
Lists sources of computer devices
and services.

**Computer Technology for the Handi-
  capped in Special Education and
  Rehabilitation**
International Council for Computers
  in Education (ICCE)
University of Oregon
1787 Agate St.
Eugene, OR 97403
(503) 686-4414

**Computers, Education and Special
  Needs**
Addison-Wesley Publishing Company
2725 Sand Hill Rd.
Menlo Park, CA 94025
(415) 854-0300
  This book provides an introduction to the use of computers by and
for people with special needs. It ex-
plores the issues central to learning — communication, access, and
motivation — and how these issues
are affected when the computer is
used as a tool in special education.

The Computing Teacher
International Council for Computers
  in Education (ICCE)
University of Oregon
Eugene, OR 97403
(503) 686-4414

Connections
Apple Computer, Inc.
20525 Mariani Ave., MS 2SE
Cupertino, CA 95014
(408) 974-7910, (408) 974-7911 (TDD)
  Connections is a guide to computer

resources for children and adults
with disabilities. The brochure is
published by Apple's Worldwide
Disability Solutions Group. *Connections* draws on Apple Computer's
compilation of the thousands of
computer resources available for
children and adults with disabilities.
Its purpose is to help the reader find
answers and explore possibilities. It
is also designed to help the user plug
into the network of specialized resources that has grown up around
the microcomputer industry.

ConnSENSE Bulletin
Connecticut Special Education Resource Center
Hartford Graduate Center
Hartford, CT 06120
(203) 246-8514
  This publication contains reviews
of software that apply to special student needs. It includes upcoming
events and descriptions and commentary on technological advances
for people with disabilities as well as
resource and reference information.

**Control of Computer-Based Technol-
  ogy for People with Physical Disabilities**
University of Toronto Press
10 St. Mary St., Suite 700
Toronto, ON M4Y 2W8
(416) 667-7791
  *Control of Computer-Based Technology
for People with Physical Disabilities* is
an assessment manual which enables
the clinician to match technological
control methods with the particular
needs of a disabled person. The
book presents a conceptual model of
the assessment process and general
procedures for the clinician to follow. The assessment protocol is

oriented towards inter-disciplinary teams. It does not involve formal, norm-referenced measures or detailed step-by-step procedures. Within the model, the clinician maintains the flexibility to modify procedures as required to meet each individual client's needs.

COPH Bulletin
Committee on Personal Computers
    and the Handicapped
2030 W. Irving Park Rd.
Chicago, IL 60618
(312) 866-8195
    This bulletin is published by an organization active in advancing the use of computer technology by individuals who are disabled.

Coping with Daily Life — Handbook of Technical Aids
Fondation Francois-Charon
525, Blvd. Hamel
Quebec G1M 2S8
(418) 529-9141
    This handbook explains how to design and build technical aids. It shows how to make more than 100 adaptations. It is a reference tool intended for people living with physical or sensory limitations, adults and children alike, and is designed to be used with people working in the field of health or education, in rehabilitation centers, in hospitals, schools or community centers.

Current Expressions
Prentke Romich Company
1022 Heyl Rd.
Wooster, OH 44691
(216) 262-1984
    This quarterly newsletter contains product information and articles about users of systems manufactured by Prentke-Romich Company, one of the leading adaptive technology companies in the nation. Prentke-Romich manufactures augmentative and assistive communication devices and the HeadMaster.

D/SNUG
The Boston Computer Society
One Center Plaza
Boston, MA 02108
(617) 367-8080
    This quarterly newsletter is published by the Boston Computer Society for the Disabled/Special Need Users Group.

Dialogue
Dialogue Publications
3100 Oak Park Ave.
Berwyn, IL 60402
    Quarterly. Available in large print, flexible disc, cassette, and Braille for $20. A general-interest publication for blind and visually impaired persons, which frequently contains articles on computer applications.

Directory of Agencies and Organizations Serving Deaf-Blind Individuals
Helen Keller National Center for
    Deaf-Blind
111 Middle Neck Rd.
Sands Point, NY 11050
(516) 944-8900
    The Directory of Agencies and Organizations Serving Deaf-Blind Individuals is designed as a resource to parents and professionals who are seeking services for persons who are deaf-blind nationwide. The directory includes federally funded, public and privately funded programs and the listing appear alphabetically according to state, city and name of agency.

The Disability Rag
The Advocado Press, Inc.
Box 145
Louisville, KY 40201
(502) 459-5343
  This contains articles, commentary, media excerpts, and letters about social policy that affect disabled children and adults and it frequently contains articles relating to technology.

Disabled USA
Presidential Committee on Employment of the Handicapped
1111 20th St. NW
Washington, DC 20036
(202) 653-5079
  This committee publishes topical articles of general interest to disabled adults and articulates the needs of the mentally and physically disabled. The goal is not only to help handicapped people adapt to society but also to convince society to adapt to the handicapped by eliminating environmental and social barriers that prevent them from living independently.

The Disseminator
Tri-Visual Services
P.O. Box 8176
Sacramento, CA 95818
(916) 441-2009
  The Disseminator is a semiannual newsletter published in January and July. The newsletter is available in large-print, braille, and cassette tape editions. It is available at no charge to subscribers.

Ed Tech News
Florida Department of Education
Educational Technology Section
Tallahassee, FL 32301
(904) 488-0980

Education Computer News
Capitol Publications
1300 N. 17th St.
Arlington, VA 22209
(703) 528-5400
  This bimonthly newsletter reports on computer advances in education, on teacher training, software purchasing, new products, research, legislation, state and local news, meetings, and conventions.

Education of the Handicapped
Capitol Publications
1300 N. 17th St.
Arlington, VA 22209
(703) 528-5400
  This bimonthly newsletter contains timely information about federal, state, and local efforts to educate handicapped children. It covers new laws and regulations, court cases, and funding.

Education Update
Association for Retarded Citizens
250 Ave. J
Arlington, TX 76006
(800) 433-5255
  This is a publication from a major association dedicated to serving the needs of disabled individuals.

Educational Technology
Educational Technology Publications
140 Sylvan Ave.
Englewood Cliffs, NJ 07632
(201) 871-4007
  This monthly publication covers the application of computers in education, literature and product reviews, and abstracts of documents from the ERIC Clearinghouse of Information Resources.

*Eighty-Eight Easy-to-Make Aids for
  Older People and for Special Needs*

Hartley & Marks, Inc.
P.O. Box 147
Point Roberts, WA 98281
(206) 945-2017

Eighty-Eight Easy-to-Make Aids for Older People and for Special Needs is a book designed to promote an enjoyable, continuing self-sufficiency for someone with a temporary or permanent disability. The book provides illustrated instructions for do-it-yourself construction of assistive devices. The projects can be made inexpensively with only basic skills, tools and materials. Some of the projects include a portable table work top, a slip-proof cutting board, loops to ease drawer opening and a garden kneeler.

Electronic Communication Aids: Selection and Use

College Hill Press/Little, Brown & Company
200 West St.
Waltham, MA 02254-9931
(617) 890-0250

This is an introductory book that provides practical information and guidelines for immediate application by the practicing professional or student. The author discusses the major features of electronic aids, compares them with electronic devices, and provides comprehensive techniques and guidelines for their selection and use.

Electronic Education: Computers in Special Education

Electronic Communications
1311 Executive Center Dr., Suite 220
Tallahassee, FL 32301
(904) 878-4178

8 issues annually, print, $18/year. Includes issues related to vision.

Electronic Learning

Scholastic, Inc.
730 Broadway
New York, NY 10003
(800) 325-6149, (212) 505-3537

This publication provides nontechnical introductions to educational computing applications. A group of educators evaluates commercial software and discusses the success of classroom applications as well as pedagogical and programming faults in the software. Regular features include a primer for teachers with minimal computer literacy, teachers' suggestions for simple computer-based classroom activities, and guides to proposal writing and funding sources.

Everybody's Technology

Charlecoms Enr.
P.O. Box 419
Montreal, ON H1S 2Z3
(514) 582-3155

More than 150 descriptions and illustrations of simple technical aids help nonspeaking people to communicate more effectively. Lists of resources, periodicals, books, articles, and distributors are also provided. This book covers portable systems, laptrays, accessing tools, and encoding techniques.

The Exceptional Parent

Psy-Ed Corporation
605 Commonwealth Ave.
Boston, MA 02215
(617) 536-8961

This bimonthly magazine contains information about federal, state, and local efforts to educate handicapped children. One issue every year is devoted to technology applications for disabled individuals.

Family Computing
Scholastic, Inc.
730 Broadway
New York, NY 10003
(800) 325-6149, (212) 505-3537
Aimed at families who have — or are contemplating purchasing — a home computer and who have children aged 5 to 15, this monthly focuses on practical information for using computers for fun and learning. Most articles address parents who are learning about computers, but some are written specifically for young people.

Family Support Bulletin
UCPA Community Services Division
1522 K St. N.W.
Washington, DC 20005
(800) 872-2827
Published by the United Cerebral Palsy Association, this quarterly newsletter contains information of interest to families with a member who has a severe disability or chronic health condition.

Financing Adaptive Technology: A Guide to Sources and Strategies for Blind and Visually Impaired Users
Smiling Interface
P.O. Box 2792 Church St. Station
New York, NY 10008-2792
(212) 222-0312
The book explains all the sources of technology funding for the vocational rehabilitation system, state agencies, the social security system, tax system, commercial credit system, governmental and nonprofit loan programs, veterans benefits and special education.

First Dibs
First DIBS, Inc.
P.O. Box 1285

Tucson, AZ 85702-1285
(602) 327-8277
First Dibs is a bimonthly publication about resources on disability and related uses. "DIBS" stands for Disability Information Brokerage System.

Focus on Technology
Telesensory Systems, Inc.
P.O. Box 7456
Mountain View, CA 94039
(415) 960-0920
Quarterly. No charge, print or cassette. Describes new TSI products and their applications.

GA-SK Newsletter
Telecommunications for the Deaf, Inc.
814 Thayer Ave.
Silver Spring, MD 20910
(301) 589-3786
GA-SK is a newsletter published quarterly by Telecommunications for the Deaf, Inc. TDI is a national nonprofit organization established with the objective of promoting telecommunications accessibility for all hearing-impaired communities.

Handbook of Microcomputer Applications in Communication Disorders
College Hill Press/Little, Brown & Company
200 West St.
Waltham, MA 02254-9931
(617) 890-0250
A book written specifically for communication disorders professionals and students, the text answers questions about choosing, buying and using computer hardware and software for clinical, research, teaching and administrative applications in speech-language pathology and audiology.

Handbook of Microcomputers in Special Education
College-Hill Press
34 Beacon St.
Boston, MA 02108
(617) 227-0730
This is a comprehensive and clearly written overview of computer applications in special education and related fields.

Harbinger
Designing Aids for Disabled Adults
1076 Bathurst St.
Toronto, ON M5R 3G9
(416) 533-4494
Harbinger is a Canadian magazine covering issues related to the use of technology by persons with physical and sensory disabilities as well as individuals with cognitive and/or developmental handicaps.

Hear-Say
Southside Virginia Training Center
P.O. Box 4110 C-37
Petersburg, VA 23832
(703) 524-7000
Hear-Say is a newsletter written for speech and language specialists. It is a reader-contributed newsletter. A subscription to *Hear-Say* is free.

Implementation Strategies for Improving the Use of Communication Aids in Schools
American Speech-Language-Hearing Association
10801 Rockville Pike
Rockville, MD 20852
(301) 897-5700
Twenty-four strategies are available for dissemination. The goal of each strategy is to provide professionals with a detailed description and/or lesson plan of effective, efficient, practical, and replicable practices used in exemplary communication aids programs.

IMS
International Marketing Services, Inc.
11 Siesta Lane
Port Richey, FL 33568
(813) 842-3231
Monthly, no charge; regular print. Manufacturer's newsletter, information on image enhancement and large print products.

InCider
InCider Publications
80 Pine St.
Peterborough, NH 03458
(603) 924-9471
This monthly magazine deals with the Apple II series of computers and includes articles and reviews on educational software.

Independence Day: Designing Computer Solutions for Individuals with a Disability
DLM Teaching Resources
P.O. Box 4000
Allen, TX 75002
(800) 527-4747, TX (800) 442-4711
This book was written primarily for individuals with a disability and for professionals in the fields of special education and rehabilitation. Through case studies and descriptions of selected adaptive products, *Independence Day* describes strategies and solutions for tailoring personal computers to meet individuals needs and objectives.

Input/Output
669 Casleton Ave.
Staten Island, NY 10301
(718) 984-1526
This periodical is published by

emotionally handicapped students in the New York City Public Schools. It serves as a clearinghouse for technology in special education.

Journal for Computer Users in Speech and Hearing
School of Speech and Hearing
  Sciences
Ohio University
Athens, OH 45701
(614) 594-6168
  This journal publishes manuscripts dealing with computer applications in diagnosis, treatment, and delivery of services to communicatively handicapped persons. It includes software/hardware reviews.

Journal of Educational Computing Research
Baywood Publishing Company, Inc.
Box D 120 Marine St.
Farmingdale, NY 11735
(516) 249-7130
  This journal is dedicated to advancing knowledge and practice in the field of educational computing. It publishes original, refereed articles on empirical research, conceptual and theoretical analyses, design and development studies, and critical reviews.

Journal of Educational Technology Systems
Baywood Publishing Company, Inc.
Box D 120 Marine St.
Farmingdale, NY 11735
(516) 249-7130
  This quarterly technical educational journal is primarily concerned with curriculum and program development. Articles discuss the models and structure inherent in educational programs and are directed toward the developers of curriculum

projects or instructional support systems.

Journal of Learning Disabilities
633 3rd Ave.
New York, NY 10017
(212) 741-5986
  This professional journal frequently includes descriptions of special software and computer applications for children with learning disabilities.

Journal of Special Education Technology
Peabody College
Vanderbilt University
Box 328
Nashville, TN 37203
No phone
  The *Journal of Special Education Technology* is a publication for the proliferation of information, research, and reports of innovative practices regarding the application of educational technology toward the development and education of exceptional children. The journal is sent to subscribers and to members of the Technology and Media Division of the Council for Exceptional Children (TAM). It is published four times a year.

Journal of Visual Impairment and Blindness
American Foundation for the Blind
15 West 16th St.
New York, NY 10011
(212) 620-2000
  10 issues/year. $25. Print, cassette, and braille formats. "Random Access" a column devoted to comparative product evaluations from the National Technology Center, plus new product announcements, training opportunities, etc.

Kurzweil Reading Machine Update
Kurzweil Computer Products
185 Albany St.
Cambridge, MA 02139
(617) 864-4700, (800) 843-0311
    Free, 2 issues per year; regular
print. News reports and the reading
machines development and utiliza-
tions at various sites.

LARGE PRINT Resource Lists
Resources for Rehabilitation
33 Bedford St.
Lexington, MA 02173
(617) 862-6455
    The *LARGE PRINT Resource Lists*
provides up-to-date information for
people with visual impairments.
Printed in 18 point bold type, the
Resource Lists is a source of information about organizations, publications, and audio-visual materials for
people with vision loss.

Link-and-Go
COPH-2
2020 Irving Park Rd.
Chicago, IL 60618
(312) 866-8195
    This periodical is dedicated to
handicapped persons who use personal computers. It contains articles
of general interest concerning the
use of microcomputers.

Living with Low Vision
Resources for Rehabilitation
33 Bedford St.
Lexington, MA 02173
(617) 862-6455
    Living with Low Vision is a series
of publications that includes large-
print resource lists, a professional
desk reference, and a large-print resource guide for individuals with vision loss. It is a directory that helps
people with vision loss (and their

family members) to locate the services they need to remain independent.

**MAINSTREAM: Magazine of the
    Able Disabled**
Exploding Myths, Inc.
2973 Beech St.
San Diego, CA 92102-7870
(619) 234-3138
    Covering independent living and
employment related technology, the
magazine has feature articles on individuals who have a handicapping
condition.

**Making an Exceptional Difference:
    Enhancing the Impact of Micro-
    computer Technology**
Exceptional Parent Press
1170 Commonwealth Ave., 3rd Fl.
Boston, MA 02134
(617) 536-8961
    This book is a collection of
articles that provide practical information about applying technology
and using computers with children
having various disabilities.

**Making Honeywell Computers Acces-
    sible to Disabled People**
Honeywell Information Systems
Publications, MS 486
200 Smith St.
Waltham, MA 02154
February 1987

**Managing End User Computing for
    Users with Disabilities**
General Services Administration
Information Resources Management
    Service
Clearinghouse on Computer Accom-
    modation
Rm. 2022, KGDO
18th & F Sts., N.W.
Washington, DC 20405
(202) 523-1906

1989. No charge. Presents guidance to Federal managers and other personnel unfamiliar with the application of computer and related information technology to accommodate users with disabilities.

The Marketplace
Council for Exceptional Children
1920 Association Dr.
Reston, VA 22091-1589
(703) 620-3660, (703) 264-9463,
(800) 873-8255
The Marketplace is a publication of the Center for Special Education Technology. The publication is geared toward publishers and provides vital marketing issues affecting special education technology products.

MCS Modem
MCS/Triformation 3132 SE Jay St.
Stuart, FL 33497
(305) 283-4817
Four to six issues per year; free, regular print. Details company's products for visually impaired computer users; commonly asked questions and answers; short new announcements.

Micro Materials Update
American Printing House for the Blind
P.O. Box 6085
Louisville, KY 40206
Quarterly, free. Available in large print or braille form. Newsletter, features innovative uses of computers, hardware updates, and user information for visually impaired computer users.

Microcomputer News for Teachers of Blind Students
517 Jasmine Rd.

St. Augustine, FL 32086
(904) 797-8621
Quarterly; regular print, $5, large print $7, Apple disc for $20 for four issues. Information about new products and other related information.

Microcomputer Resource Book for Special Education
Reston Publishing Co.
Reston, VA
Dolores Hagen. 1984. 224 pages. $15.95.

Microcomputers in Special Education
Brookline Books
P.O. Box 1046-A
Cambridge, MA 02238
(617) 868-0360
This book introduces special educators and administrators to the computer as an instructional tool. It includes a discussion of the origins and basic operation of computers as well as practical advice on using computer assisted instruction and on evaluating and selecting appropriate educational software.

Microcomputers in the Schools — Implementation in Special Education
SRA Technologies
901 S. Highland St.
Arlington, VA 22204
Tom Hanley.

MICRO-SCOPE
Exceptional Children's Software
P.O. Box 487
Hays, KS 67601
(913) 625-9281
This quarterly newsletter addresses topical issues relating to disabled children and technology. It often contains articles written by disabled children. The periodical

also contains articles of general interest concerning the use of microcomputers.

Mindscape Methods for Mastery
Mindscape, Inc.
Dept. SE
Northbrook, IL 60062
(800) 221-9884

Mindscape Methods for Mastery matches the Mindscape software titles to 120 academic and social skills of special relevance to students with special learning needs. Each software title is cross-referenced for introducing, practicing, and reinforcing instruction in reading, reasoning, and expressing.

Moving Forward
P.O. Box 1304
La Canada, CA 91011
(818) 952-1340

This publication contains articles on various disabilities. It also contains regular items on computer technology.

NARIC Resource Guides
National Rehabilitation Information
  Center
8455 Colesville Rd., Suite 935
Silver Spring, MD 20910-3319
(800) 346-2742

NARIC has begun producing a series of resource guides as general resources for persons desiring basic information about a disability or related area. The guides are distributed free of charge. The first three guides cover the topics: traumatic brain injury, spinal cord injury and families and disability.

Network
Minnesota Educational Computing
  Consortium

3490 Lexington Ave. North
Minneapolis, MN 55126
(612) 481-3500, (800) 228-3504

Bimonthly, free; regular print. Instructional newsletter listing materials.

The Networker
UCPA Community Services Division
1522 K St. N.W.
Washington, DC 20005
(800) 872-2827

The Networker is a quarterly publication of the United Cerebral Palsy Association. The newsletter is part of a continuing and expanding effort of UCPA's Community Services Division to provide support and leadership to state and local UCPA affiliates.

New Information Technology in the
  Education of Disabled Children
  and Adults
College-Hill Press
34 Beacon St.
Boston, MA 02108
(617) 227-0730

Beginning with an assessment of the learning problems faced by disabled people, this book reviews the scope of new information technology and discusses how computers are being used in the education of students of all ages.

Newsounds
Alexander Graham Bell Association
  for the Deaf
3417 Volta Place NW
Washington, DC 20007
(202) 337-5220

This newsletter for deaf and hearing-impaired individuals is published alternately with the *Volta Review*. It contains information on

conferences concerning microcomputers.

On-Line Today
COMPUSERVE, Inc.
5000 Arlington Centre Blvd.
Columbus, OH 43220
(800) 848-8990
   This periodical informs subscribers to COMPUSERVE's Handicapped Users' Database about new
technologies and services available
on the database.

Options
Life Options
P.O. Box 206
Wilmington, NC 28402
(919) 343-9931
   Options is a magazine published to
offer readers who are visually impaired or blind a way through a
myriad of related products. In addition to offering new software and
hardware for computer users and
consumers, the magazine has a section that highlights items readers
don't need or can't use anymore
(e.g., magnifiers, braillers, speech
synthesizers) that only another person who is blind might want or
need.

Paraplegia News
5201 N. 19th Ave. 111
Phoenix, AZ 85015
(602) 246-9426
   This publication offers information on a variety of issues related to
spinal cord injury. It includes articles on accessibility, research,
recreation, legislation, and new
products.

PEOPLENET
257 Center Lane

Levittown, NY 11756
No phone
   This quarterly personals print
newsletter is composed of 50-word
descriptions of interesting men and
women with disabilities. For additional information, send a self-
addressed, stamped, business-size
envelope to *PEOPLENET.*

*Personal Computer Opportunities for
   the Handicapped Newsletter*
Personal Computer Opportunities
   for the Handicapped
P.O. Box 374
Spicer, MN 56288
(612) 796-5765
   This periodical is for disabled persons who are trying to acquire job
skills with the help of a computer.

*Personal Computers and Special
   Needs*
SYBEX, Inc.
2344 Sixth St.
Berkeley, CA 94710
(415) 548-4500
   This book explains how computers may be used to monitor
home security, produce synthesized
speech, summon emergency medical
assistance, conduct banking and on-
line shopping, and perform as an
education aid for dyslexic children.

Personal Computers and the Disabled
Quantum Press
Doubleday & Company
Garden City, NY
   Peter McWilliams. October 1984.
416 pages. $9.95.

Personal Computing
Hayden Publishing Company
50 Essex St.
Rochelle Park, NJ 07662
(201) 843-0550

This monthly publication contains product reviews and listings, in addition to general editorial content. Oriented toward home and business microcomputing the monthly deals with programming applications and hardware.

Planning and Implementing Augmentative Communication Service Delivery
RESNA
Suite 700
Washington, DC 20036
(202) 857-1199
Planning and Implementing Augmentative Communication Service Delivery is a book about the issues and problems related to providing, in an educational setting, appropriate rehabilitation services to individuals with communication and/or mobility disabilities. The book provides an overview of the issues that state and other agencies must address; examples of planning and of effective service delivery models based on cooperative efforts among a variety of individuals; and an overview of the acquisition of funds. The technology discussed in this book includes communication devices, mobility devices, environmental control systems and computer modifications.

A Pocket Guide to Federal Help for the Disabled Person
Consumer Information Center
P.O. Box 100
Pueblo, CO 81002
(719) 948-3334
A Pocket Guide to Federal Help for the Disabled Person is a list of federally funded programs, including those involving vocational rehabilitation, health care, and housing.

Quick Guide to Resources in Special Education Technology
San Mateo County Office of Education
Special Education Division
Redwood City, CA 94063
(415) 363-5476
The guide includes annotated lists of organizations, associations, government agencies, producers of software and adaptive devices, publications, directories, periodicals, journals, networks, and software evaluation sources.

Raised Dot Computing Newsletter
Raised Dot Computing
408 S. Baldwin
Madison, WI 53703
(608) 257-9595
This periodical describes microcomputer resources and related information appropriate to visually impaired or blind individuals. Raised Dot Computing is the manufacturer of braille editing software.

Rehab/Education ResourceBook
series
Trace Center
S-151 Waisman Center
University of Wisconsin
Madison, WI 53705
(608) 262-6966
Trace ResourceBook 1989–90 Edition, 798 pages, $49. The Communication, Control, and Computer Access for Disabled and Elderly Individuals Series included: *ResourceBook 1: Communication Aids, ResourceBook 2: Switches and Environmental Controls, ResourceBook 3: Hardware and Software,* and *ResourceBook 4: Update to Books 1, 2 and 3.* The 1989–90 edition updates and consolidates the previous 4 books into 1 volume. A cross-referenced registry of communica-

tion aids, training aids, switches, environmental control systems, software, and hardware modifications created or adapted for individuals with disabilities. Extensive resource lists in Appendix. Good glossary. Also available in electronic form as Hyper-TraceBase.

Rehabilitation Gazette
Gazette International Networking
 Institute
4502 Maryland Ave.
St. Louis, MO 63108
(314) 361-0475
 This biannual international journal is on the subject of independent living. Published by disabled individuals, it features book reviews, discussions of technological equipment, and articles on disabled people around the world.

Rehabilitation Resource Manual
Resources for Rehabilitation
33 Bedford St.
Lexington, MA 02173
(617) 862-6455
 Rehabilitation Resource Manual is a professional desk reference with referral guidelines, a bibliography, and a list of resources for those who want to guide individuals with vision loss to appropriate rehabilitation services.

**Rehabilitation Technology Resource
 Guide**
Human Interaction Research Institute
1849 Sawtelle Blvd., Suite 102
Los Angeles, CA 90025
(213) 479-3028
 The *Rehabilitation Technology Resource Guide* provides a listing of information centers, particularly those that have searchable databases and referral services. The guide in-

cludes listings for technology relevant to all types of disabilities and is published in looseleaf notebook form so that it can be regularly updated.

Rehabilitation Technology Review
RESNA
Suite 700
Washington, DC 20036
(202) 857-1199
 This is the professional newsletter of rehabilitation engineering. RESNA is the primary professional organization for individuals interested in the advancement of the rehabilitation sciences.

**Rehabilitation Technology Service
 Delivery: A Practical Guide**
RESNA
Suite 700
Washington, DC 20036
(202) 857-1199
 Rehabilitation Technology Service Delivery: A Practical Guide is about program building and guides the reader through a variety of strategies for operating successful service delivery programs for adaptive equipment. Chapters on service delivery models, marketing, development and implementation, business practices, funding and additional resources have been contributed by writers who explain how they planned, developed and implemented workable programs and how they identified and avoided the pitfalls.

Resource Guide for School Psychologists
Planet Press
P.O. Box 3477
Newport Beach, CA 92663-3418
(714) 650-5135
 This guide is a 20-page listing of

the major resources (conferences, newsletters, organizations, bulletin boards), software programs, and companies. It covers intellectual, vocational, personality, adaptive behavior, IEP, behavioral intervention, and management software.

Resource Guide for Transition Materials from School to Work
The Conover Company
P.O. Box 155
Omro, WI 54963
(414) 231-4667
   A free guide from The Conover Company, this guide presents programs for daily living, including vocational assessment, career planning, center guidance, survival skills, vocational training, and social skills. Many of the programs were developed by the National Center for Research in Vocational Education at Ohio State University.

Resource Inventories
Council for Exceptional Children
1920 Association Dr.
Reston, VA 22091-1589
(703) 620-3660, (703) 264-9463,
   (800) 873-8255
   Resource Inventories are publications of the Center for Special Education Technology which list technology resources on a state or national basis. These 2 to 5 page inventories are available for 48 states and for topical areas such as assistive technology and national information centers.

Resource Manual
The Carroll Center for the Blind
770 Centre St.
Newton, MA 02158-2597
(617) 969-6200
   This manual is a summary of

techniques used in the model programs of the Carroll Center for the Blind.

Rural Special Education Technology
National Rural Development Institute
359 Miller Hall
Bellingham, WA 98225
(206) 676-3576
   Each issue contains resources and problem-solving strategies. Many of the topics covered are related to technology for handicapped persons. The periodical also contains articles of general interest concerning the use of microcomputers.

Ruralink
ACRES
359 Miller Hall
Bellingham, WA 98225
(206) 676-3576
   Each issue of this publication contains a section on technology. Various other sections report on the latest technological and adaptive devices for rural disabled individuals.

SAF Quarterly Journal
Sensory Aids Foundation
399 Sherman Ave.
Palo Alto, CA 94306
(415) 329-0430
   The purpose of the Sensory Aids Foundation is to explore the use of technological aids to assist visually-impaired and hearing-impaired persons. The journal is published to report on innovative SAF projects.

SAF Technology Update
Sensory Aids Foundation (SAF)
399 Sherman Ave.
Palo Alto, VA 94306
(415) 329-0430

See *Sensus* (below), monthly, regular print, tape. A newsletter that gives capsule reports on issues, projects, training programs, products, and publications. Subscription to *Technology Update* is included with subscription for *Sensus.*

SAINT
Leaders Digest, Inc.
6803 Whittier Ave.
McLean, VA 22101
(703) 442-8780

SAINT (Special and Individual Needs Technology) is a monthly, consumer-oriented newsletter aimed at enriching the lives of people with special needs. The newsletter provides information to assist people in achieving personal independence.

SchoolTech News
Education News Service
P.O. Box 1789
Carmichael, CA 95609
(916) 483-6159

This newsletter is published 7 times a year to report on significant new developments in educational technology. It includes research findings, software reviews, and successful uses of computers in education.

Second Beginner's Guide to Personal Computers for the Blind and Visually Impaired
National Braille Press, Inc.
88 Saint Stephens St.
Boston, MA 02115
(617) 266-6160

Written by blind users, the *Beginner's Guide* includes a buyer's guide to talking computers and large print display processors. It also contains information about training programs across the country.

Section 508: Access to Information Technology
General Services Administration (GSA)
KGDO, 18th and F. St. N.W., Rm. 2022
Washington, DC 20405
(202) 523-1906

In 1986, Congress authorized an amended version of the Rehabilitation Act of 1973. Section 508, as incorporated into the Act, mandates that guidelines be established to ensure that individuals who have a disability are able to use electronic office equipment, with or without special hardware or software, and agencies comply with these guidelines in the purchase or lease of electronic office equipment. The guidelines outline management responsibilities and functional specifications. The guidelines state that agency managers should ensure that the requirements of individuals with disability are identified during the procurement planning phase. In outlining functional specifications, three major areas—input, output and documentation—must be addressed during the planning for and procurement of electronic office equipment.

Selecting Access Systems for Individuals with Physical Disabilities
Hugh MacMillan Medical Centre
350 Rumsey Rd.
Toronto, ON M4G 1R8
(416) 425-6220

Selecting Access Systems for Individuals with Physical Disabilities is a clinical resource manual for the systematic assessment of alternate access methods for people with physical disabilities.

Sensory Aids Foundation Newsletter
HumanWare, Inc.
6245 King Rd., Suite P
Loomis, CA 95650
(916) 652-7253
This is a bimonthly newsletter for deaf, blind, and visually impaired individuals. The newsletter is also available on cassette.

Sensory Aids Report
Sensory Aids Corporation
205 West Grand Ave., Suite 122
Bensenville, IL 60106
(800) 722-3393
Quarterly, free, print. Manufacturer's letter.

Sensus
Sensory Aids Foundation
399 Sherman Ave.
Palo Alto, CA 94306
(415) 329-0430
This quarterly guide provides in-depth, critical reviews of sensory aids. The guide also contains articles of general interest concerning the use of microcomputers.

SENSUS Technology Update
HumanWare, Inc.
6245 King Rd., Suite P
Loomis, CA 95650
(916) 652-7253
This guide contains a sensory aids technology update. The publisher also manufactures a number of special education and rehabilitation products.

SERC Newsletter
Connecticut Special Education Resource Center
Harford Graduate Center
Hartford, CT 06120
(203) 246-8514
Outlining in-service activities and listing new acquisitions, including professional books, instructional materials, and microcomputers, this newsletter also contains articles of general interest concerning the use of microcomputers.

Sibs
Sibs Publishing Co.
15 Barnes Circle
Salem, MA 01970
No phone
Sibs is a magazine for siblings of people with developmental, psychological, physical, and/or cosmetic disorders. Through its editorials and articles, *Sibs* aims to explore all the emotional aspects involved with being the sibling of a mentally or physically challenged person.

SIG Bulletin
International Council for Computers in Education (ICCE)
University of Oregon
Eugene, OR 97403
(503) 686-4414
A quarterly forum for ICCE special interest groups (SIG); one SIG is the SIGSPED for Special Education. The bulletin also contains articles of general interest concerning the use of microcomputers.

SIGCAPH Newsletter
SIGCAPH (Special Interest Group on Computers and the Physically Handicapped
11 West 42nd St.
New York, NY 10036
Quarterly, $22/year, regular print, tape. Promotes professional interests of computing personnel with physical disabilities. Special interest group seeks solutions to disability related problems through computer technology.

The Sloane Report
P.O. Box 561689
Miami, FL 33256
(305) 251-2199

This catalog contains a list of public domain software; 1500 programs are Apple programs. The list includes over 500 "talking" programs specifically for blind and visually impaired users.

Smith-Kettlewell Technical File
The Smith-Kettlewell Eye Research
  Institute
2232 Webster St.
San Francisco, CA 94415
(415) 561-1619

Quarterly. Braille, $18/year; diskette (ASCII file) $16/year; talking book format, $14/year. No print form available.

Software in the Classroom: A Newsletter
Focus Media, Inc.
839 Stewart Ave.
Garden City, NY 11530
(800) 645-8989

This newsletter contains a list of educational software that may be of interest to special education teachers and rehabilitation professionals.

Speak Out
CT Parent Advocacy Center
Mohegan Community College
Norwich, CT 06360
(203) 886-5250

This bimonthly newsletter provides information about programs, services, and legislation related to handicapped children and their families.

Special Education and Rehabilitation Software Catalog
Intuit Computing

1915 Huguenot Rd.
Richmond, VA 23235
(804) 379-2253

This catalog contains a list of over 100 software programs that can be used in special education and rehabilitation programs. The programs are grouped in the following categories: Language, Arithmetic, Reasoning, Activities of Daily Living, Health, Productivity, Art Tools, Computer Literacy, Map Skills, Music and Memory.

Special Education Technology Newsletter
Pearl Creek Elementary
P.O. Box 1250
Fairbanks, AK 99707
(907) 479-4234

Practicing special education teachers publish a newsletter about classroom and therapy issues. The newsletter contains software and hardware reviews, case studies, and current research.

The Special Educator
CRR Publishing Company
421 King St.
Alexandria, VA 22313-1905
(703) 684-0510

A review of events of interest to special educators, the publication also contains articles on computer technology and the special education student.

Special Magic
Mayfield Publishing Co.
1240 Villa St.
Mountain View, CA 94041
(415) 960-3222

An overview of computers in special education settings, this text was designed for both novices and experts. The book covers topics such

as getting a computer into the classroom, selecting software, instructional applications, music and art,
LOGO, social development, disability categories, computer-
generated IEPs, and a variety of
related practices and applications. It
includes case studies, examples of
instructional activities, organizational strategies, and lists of resources.

Spectrum

The Center for Rehabilitation Technology Services
1410-C Boston Ave.
P.O. Box 15
West Columbia, SC 29171-0015
(803) 739-5362

Spectrum is a newsletter published
by the Center for Rehabilitation
Technology Services. It reports news
of the center's activities. In addition
it provides information on the
trends and issues affecting the
delivery of assistive technology services. The purpose of the publication is to stimulate the increased use
of appropriate technology and to
promote improved communication
and interaction among all service
providers and users of assistive
technology.

The Speech and Hearing Newsletter

19, Continental Chambers
Pune 411 004
ID, India
No phone

An international quarterly published in India, it focuses on communication aids, therapy techniques, and research. It is intended
for anyone interested in the field of
communication sciences, from users
of communication aids to physicians
and parents.

Spinal Network

P.O. Box 4162
Boulder, CO 80306
(800) 338-5412

A "whole earth catalogue" with information for people concerned with
spinal cord injuries, this book covers
topics such as medicine, sports and
recreation, travel, media and images, computers, sex and romance,
and rights, legal and financial.

Straight-Talk

Digital Equipment Corporation
P.O. Box 190
Maynard, MA 17754
(617) 493-3113, (800) 832-6277

Regular print. Company publication about DECtalk products.

Tactic: Technology for the Visually Impaired

Clovernook Printing House for the
  Blind
600 Hamilton Ave.
Cincinnati, OH 45231
(513) 522-3860

Quarterly, Braille, $10/year.

The Tattler

Tell 'em Ware
1714 Olson Way
Marshalltown, IA 50518
(515) 752-9667

The *Special Needs Computing Newsletter* is a newsletter specifically for
special needs computer users and
their families and/or support teams.
It is published quarterly and is
available as a subscription. The
newsletter contains information on
training sources, software, new
products, conferences and public domain software.

TECH.LINE

Council for Exceptional Children

1920 Association Dr.
Reston, VA 22091-1589
(703) 620-3660, (703) 264-9463,
(800) 873-8255

The *TECH.LINE* is an electronic
newsletter appearing on SpecialNet
(SpecialNet ID: TECH. CENTER).
It is posted by the Center for
Special Education Technology at the
Council for Exceptional Children
and appears bimonthly. The use of
telecommunication allows for the
dissemination of information in a
most timely manner. The information is in the public domain and can
be copied and shared as long as the
Center is credited.

Tech Use Guides
Council for Exceptional Children
1920 Association Dr.
Reston, VA 22091-1589
(703) 620-3660, (703) 264-9463,
(800) 873-8255

Tech Use Guides are 2 to 6 page
summaries of important areas in the
use of technology in special education. The guides are published by
the Center for Special Education
Technology. Over 15 guides are currently available on topics ranging
from "Computers and Writing" to a
"Teacher's Guide" to "Learning Disabilities."

Technical Innovation Bulletin
Innovation Rehabilitation Technology, Inc.
429 Castro St.
Mountain View, CA 94941
(415) 961-3161

Six to eight issues per year, $25/
year, tape. In-depth interviews with
developers of new devices are presented on tape.

Technology & Disability
Andover Medical Publishers, Inc.
P.O. Box 1977
Andover, MA 01810
(617) 942-1438

Technology & Disability is a journal
concerning the interface of technology — particularly rehabilitative and
assistive technology — with disability.
It is published quarterly as a mono-
graph (each issue will focus on one
specific topic). The technology focus
includes low and high technology
devices used to improve function in
major life roles including medical
and community settings. Emphasis
is on assistive technology applied to
education and employment.

**Technology for Persons with Disabil-
ities, Technology for Persons with
Vision Impairments, Technology
for Persons with Hearing Impairments**
IBM National Support Center for
  Persons with Disabilities
4111 Northside Pkwy.
Atlanta, GA 30327
(800) IBM-2133 (voice or TDD),
  (404) 238-8000, (404) 238-3521
  (TDD)

Regularly updated resource directories. This free information service
can also provide product information on a whole range of hardware
and software, not just IBM products.

Technology Update
Sensory Aids Foundation
399 Sherman Ave.
Palo Alto, CA 94306
(415) 329-0430

This monthly newsletter provides
current information on developments in technology for blind and
partially sighted persons.

Technology's Edge
Triformation Systems, Inc.
3132 South East Jay St.
Stuart, FL 33494
   Quarterly, free, regular print.
Manufacturer's newsletter.

Their World
Foundation for Children with
   Learning Disabilities (FCLD)
Box 2929 Grand Central Station
New York, NY 10163
(212) 687-7211
   This publication contains stories
about the ways families cope with a
learning disabled child.

Toward Independence
Apple Computer, Inc.
20525 Mariani Ave., MS 2SE
Cupertino, CA 95014
(408) 974-7910, (408) 974-7911 (TDD)
   Toward Independence is a publication of Apple's Worldwide Disability
Solutions Group. The publication
contains information on products
that make the Macintosh accessible
to computer users who are disabled.
Toward Independence is intended as a
reference for those wishing to evaluate the Macintosh computer in ac-
cordance with the federal guidelines
mandated by Section 508 or the
Rehabilitation Act of 1973. It describes the built-in accessibility
features of the Macintosh and the
third-party products that further extend its functionality to disabled
users.

*Toys Help: A Guide to Choosing
   Toys for Handicapped Children*
Publishing & Printing Services
25 Planchet Rd.
Maple, ON L0J 1E0
No phone
   The Canadian Association of Toy

Libraries, with a grant from the
Hospital for Sick Children, published
this portfolio in 1981. It includes
Why Toys Help; Selection Criteria;
A Chart of Selected Toys and Re-
lated Skills; Organization and a Toy
Lending System; and Special Toys
for the Handicapped Child.

*TRAINING: The Magazine of
   Human Resource Development*
Lakewood Publications, Inc.
50 S. 9th St.
Minneapolis, MN 55402
(612) 333-0471
   This magazine focuses on training
disabled employees for jobs in corporate and industrial settings as well
as on making jobs accessible to disabled people. It concentrates on
adapting existing business equipment to meet the needs of disabled
individuals.

*Training and Technology for the
   Disabled: 1986*
Materials Development Center
Stout Vocational Rehabilitation Institute
Menomonie, WI 54751
(715) 232-2195
   These papers were presented at
the Discovery '86 conference, covering computer-related aspects of rehabilitation, biomedicine, environmental control, transportation, and
communication.

*Travel for the Disabled (A Handbook
   of Travel Resources and 500
   Worldwide Access)*
The Disability Bookshop
P.O. Box 129
Vancouver, WA 98666
(206) 694-2462
   This is a 92-page guide to hotels,

motels and other facilities that have limited or no mobility barriers.

UPDATE
National Institute of Dyslexia
3200 Woodbine St.
Chevy Chase, MD 20815
(301) 652-0760

This is a quarterly newsletter designed to provide summary, synthesis and, where possible, analysis of new and developing information specific to learning disabilities and dyslexia.

Using Microcomputers in Classroom Settings
DLM Teaching Resources
P.O. Box 4000
Allen, TX 75002
(800) 527-4747, TX (800) 442-4711

This pamphlet contains answers to a collection of questions asked by teachers who are working with computers in their classrooms. The answers are designed to provide ideas and practical guidelines to help teachers integrate computers into their curricula. It includes questions related to using computers with children who have special needs.

Versanews
David Goldstein, Editor
87 Sandford Lane
Stamford, CT 06905

Quarterly, $20/year. Available on VersaBraille tape or in print. Presents applications of the VersaBraille and related technologies; focuses as a VersaBraille user's group, members share information about computerized braille devices and other related topics.

VIDPI Views
Jim Fleming

5021 Seminary Rd., Apt. 1506
Alexandria, VA 22311

Quarterly, tape cassette. A subscription to *VIDPI Views* is included with the $20 membership fee in Visually Impaired Data Processors International. *VIDPI* members include students, data processing professionals, programmers, employers, instructors, and manufacturers of equipment. *VIDPI* advocates for high standards in training of qualified blind persons and promotion of employment opportunities in industry and government. It provides for the exchange of employment-related techniques and works to enhance the availability of Braille and recorded documentation in the field.

Viewpoint
Association of Rehabilitiation Programs in Data Processing
Center for Information Resources
Philadelphia, PA 19104-3054
(215) 898-8108

This publication is for individuals interested in training and placement of handicapped persons in the area of data processing. It also contains articles of general interest concerning the use of microcomputers.

Volta Review
Alexander Graham Bell Association for the Deaf
3417 Volta Place NW
Washington, DC 20007
(202) 337-5220

This journal for hearing impaired people reports on a variety of technology related topics and issues.

VTEK RE News
VTEK
1610 26th St.

students about the Law School Aptitude Test and other realities of law school life.

The Office for Civil Rights, U.S. Department of Education, maintains ten regional offices which would be able to answer questions on matters related to Section 504 of the Rehabilitation Act of 1973. For further information, contact the appropriate regional offices listed below.

Region I: (Connecticut, Maine, Massachusetts, New Hampshire, Rhode Island, Vermont)
U.S. Department of Education
Office for Civil Rights
J. W. McCormack Post Office and Courthouse Bldg., Rm. 222, 01-0061
Boston, MA 02109-4557
(617) 223-9662, (617) 223-9695 (TDD)

Region II: (New Jersey, New York, Puerto Rico, Virgin Islands)
U.S. Department of Education
Office for Civil Rights
26 Federal Plaza, 33rd Fl., Rm. 33-130, 02-1010
New York, NY 10278-0082
(212) 264-4663, (212) 264-9464 (TDD)

Region III: (Delaware, District of Columbia, Maryland, Pennsylvania, Virginia, West Virginia)
U.S. Department of Education
Office for Civil Rights
3535 Market St., Rm. 6300, 03-2010
Philadelphia, PA 19104-3326
(215) 596-6772, (215) 596-6794 (TDD)

Region IV: (Alabama, Florida, Georgia, Kentucky, Mississippi, North Carolina, South Carolina, Tennessee)
U.S. Department of Education
Office for Civil Rights
101 Marietta Tower, 27th Fl., Suite 2702
P.O. Box 1705, 04-3010
Atlanta, GA 30301-1705
(404) 331-2954, (404) 331-7816 (TDD)

Region V: (Illinois, Indiana, Michigan, Minnesota, Ohio, Wisconsin)
U.S. Department of Education
Office for Civil Rights
401 South State St., Rm. 700C, 05-4010
Chicago, IL 60606-1202
(312) 886-3456, (312) 353-2541 (TDD)

Region VI: (Arkansas, Louisiana, New Mexico, Oklahoma, Texas)
U.S. Department of Education
Office for Civil Rights
1200 Main Tower Bldg., Suite 2260, 06-5010
Dallas, TX 75202-9998
(214) 767-3959, (214) 767-3639 (TDD)

Region VII: (Iowa, Kansas, Missouri, Nebraska)
U.S. Department of Education
Office for Civil Rights
10220 N. Executive Hills Blvd., 8th Fl., 07-6010
Kansas City, MO 64153-1367
(816) 374-6461 (TDD)

Region VIII: (Colorado, Montana, North Dakota, South Dakota, Utah, Wyoming)
U.S. Department of Education
Office for Civil Rights
Federal Office Bldg.

1961 Stout St., Rm. 342, 08-7010
Denver, CO 80294-3608
(303) 844-5695, (303) 844-3417
(TDD)

Region IX: (Arizona, California, Hawaii, Nevada, Guam, Trust Territory of Pacific Islands, American Samoa)
U.S. Department of Education
Office for Civil Rights
Old Federal Bldg.
50 United Nations Plaza, Rm. 239, 09-8010
San Francisco, CA 94102
(415) 556-7000, (415) 556-6770
(TDD)

Region X: (Alaska, Idaho, Oregon, Washington)
U.S. Department of Education
Office for Civil Rights
915 Second Ave., Rm. 3310, 10-9010
Seattle, WA 98174-1099

(206) 442-6811, (206) 442-4542
(TDD)

Public Interest Law Center of Philadelphia (PILCOP)
125 South 9th St., Suite 700
Philadelphia, PA 19107
(215) 627-7100
PILCOP is a non-profit, public interest law firm with a Disabilities Project specializing in class action suits brought by individuals and organizations. The primary interests of the Disabilities Project are in promoting home and community-based support services for people with developmental disabilities and in promoting state-of-the-art education and related services for people with handicaps in integrated settings in the public schools. Higher education and employment rights of people with disabilities is another focus. (PILCOP does not deal with mental health issues.)

Appendix G:
Networks

APPLE Bulletin Board
Apple Computer, Inc.
20525 Mariani Ave., MS 2SE
Cupertino, CA 95014
(408) 974-7910, (408) 974-7911 (TDD)
The APPLE Bulletin Board provides a 24-hour-a-day forum on SpecialNet. The board provides users of SpecialNet with the opportunity to request and exchange information. APPLE is maintained by Apple Computer's Worldwide Disability Solutions Group.

BlindNet
Sensory Aids Foundation
399 Sherman Ave.
Palo Alto, CA 94306
(415) 329-0430
BlindNet is a bulletin board on WELLNET. Access WELLNET at (415) 323-1062. BlindNet and WELLNET are funded in part by a grant from the Apple Community Affairs Program.

California Information Network
Special Education Division
California State Dept. of Education
Sacramento, CA 94244-2720
(916) 323-4784
The California Information Network on SpecialNet is a total communication and information service dedicated to the state's special education community. The service is managed by the Special Education Division, California State Department of Education with assistance from Resources in Special Education. The service provides three dynamic capabilities: communication, database, and bulletin boards.

Computer Use in Social Services (CUSS)
Computer Use in Social Services
Network
The University of Texas at Arlington
Arlington, TX 76019-0129
(817) 265-0459
CUSS is a nonprofit association of professionals interested in exchanging information and experiences on the use of computers in the social services. The network contains four nodes that have a specialty focus in special education and rehabilitation.

Data Referral Network
Mobility Special Services, Inc.
190 Sumner St.
Boston, MA 02062
(617) 891-8858, NY (800) 962-1480, ext. 333
The Data Referral Network provides "one-stop shopping" for disabled individuals.

DCI DEAFNET
International Communications
  Limited
P.O. Box 81
Fayville, MA 01745
(617) 620-1777
  DCI DEAFNET is a nonprofit
organization that serves groups of
deaf users, schools with programs
for deaf students, and hearing people who have an interest in the deaf
community (either professionally or
socially). It has organized a nationwide electronic mail service with international links for deaf people.
The service uses Telemail.

The DD Connection
Association for Retarded Citizens
250 Ave. J
Arlington, TX 76006
(800) 433-5255
  The DD Connection is an electronic mail and bulletin board
system that offers service providers,
administrators, parents and persons
with disabilities a communication
forum for sharing problems, finding
solutions and exchanging ideas. A
main objective of The DD Connection is to pool information about the
use of advanced technology and assistive devices with persons who are
disabled. The DD Connection is
operated 24 hours a day and is on
the 5,300 node worldwide OPUS
Network system.

**Division of Rehabilitation Services
  (TN)**
400 Deaderick St.
Nashville, TN 37219
(615) 741-5644
  The Division of Rehabilitation
Services is on-line on SpecialNet,
RehabNet, DeafNet, SCAN, HEX
and ABLEDATA. It provides state-
wide staff training on the uses of

microcomputers in rehabilitation by
Vocational Rehabilitation counselors.

4-Sights
Greater Detroit Society for the Blind
16625 Grand River Ave.
Detroit, MI 48227
(313) 272-3900
  The 4-Sights Network is a national computer telecommunications
system for the blind, the visually impaired, and for those who work with
the blind and visually impaired.

**GEnie: The Public Forum*Non-
  Profit Connection**
GE Consumer Services
Department 02B
Rockville, MD 20850
(800) 638-9636
  The Public Forum*NonProfit
Connection is a GEnie service that
focuses on current events, news and
issues of interest to the public sector. Its RoundTable gives people in
and out of the nonprofit world a
place to exchange facts and opinions
on a range of subjects.

I-BUG
National Association of Blind and
  Visually Impaired Computer
  Users
P.O. Box 1352
Roseville, CA 95661-1352
(916) 786-3923
  I-BUG acts as the liaison between
blind users and other interested par-
ties and assists those interested in
starting their own local chapters of
I-BUG. I-BUG maintains a data-
base of resources and an electronic
bulletin board.

National Parent Chain, Inc.
867C High St.
Worthington, OH 43805
(614) 431-1911

to the educational needs of people with disabilities is available from the Assistive Device Resource Center.

Canadian Database for Educational Software
Council of Ministers of Education
252 Bloor St., West
Toronto, ON M5S 1V5
(416) 964-2781

This database provides educators with descriptive and evaluative information on microcomputer software currently available. The database offers full bilingual capabilities, instant access, and retrieval by subject.

CHID
Combined Health Information
  Database
2115 East Jefferson
Rockville, MD 20852
(301) 468-2162

Both health education and disabling conditions are given coverage in this wide-ranging database. Articles, books, unpublished documents, and program information are included.

CompuHelp
National Association of Blind and
  Visually Impaired Computer
  Users
P.O. Box 1352
Roseville, CA 95661-1352
(916) 786-3923

The National Association of Blind and Visually Impaired Computer Users, a nonprofit, charitable corporation, has installed a database called CompuHelp for use by persons who are blind or visually impaired. The database can be reached 24 hours a day (via a modem) by calling (916) 786-3923. The database is a menu driven bulletin board

system. A caller can find information pertaining to computer hardware, software, self-help groups, and publications. The database is available on disk.

CompuPlay Software Database for Young Children with Special Needs
National Lekotek Center
2100 Ridge Ave.
Evanston, IL 60204
(312) 328-0001

The CompuPlay database is the result of a study of software related to children with special needs. It is intended to be a guide for the selection of software appropriate for children with mental, physical, behavioral, sensory, and learning impairments. Suggestions for gifted children are also included. The database is updated bimonthly and includes over 85 software programs that have been used with children with special needs ranging in age from 2–14.

The Developmental Disabilities Technology Library
Association for Retarded Citizens
250 Avenue J
Arlington, TX 76006
(800) 433-5255

The Developmental Disabilities Technology Library (DDTL) is a computerized database of information on the application of advanced technology and assistive devices with children and adults who are disabled. The DDTL contains information about technology and assistive devices for persons with disabilities in the following four categories: publications; authorities on the use of various assistive devices and actual users of devices; resource agencies and vendors of assistive devices. The DDTL is accessible to a subscriber who logs onto the DD Connection's electronic mail and bulletin board system.

ECER
Council for Exceptional Children
1920 Association Dr.
Reston, VA 22091-1589
(703) 620-3660, (703) 264-9463,
  (800) 873-8255
ECER is the ERIC clearinghouse database for the disability field. It contains bibliographic information on books, articles, teaching materials, and reports on the education of handicapped and gifted children.

ERIC
Council for Exceptional Children
1920 Association Dr.
Reston, VA 22091-1589
(703) 620-3660, (703) 264-9463,
  (800) 873-8255
ERIC is an on-line information source maintained on Dialog. The service is available to anyone who has access to a modem and a computer terminal, communicating word processor or personal computer with terminal software. Users can order complete printed documents and articles while on-line.

HyperAbleData
Trace Center
S-151 Waisman Center
Madison, WI 53705
(608) 262-6966
HyperAbleData is a HyperCard stack of over 13,000 commercially available products designed for persons with functional limitations.

**Information Center for Special
  Education Media and Materials**

LINC Resources, Inc.
3857 North High St.
Columbus, OH 43214
(614) 263-5462
Educators, researchers/developers, publishers/distributors, and others can use the center's database as well as obtain information on marketing and legal issues, market trends, and issues effecting special education. In addition, the center will provide help in locating nonprofit special education publishers and placing "thin market" materials.

National Clearinghouse on Technology and Aging
University Center on Aging
University of Massachusetts Medical
  Center
Worcester, MA 01655
(617) 856-6506
The National Clearinghouse on Technology and Aging includes documents, audio-visual materials, catalogs, an expert network referral database, funding resource database, prototypes, graphic designs, and the Sensory Technology Information Service database.

National Technology Center
American Foundation for the Blind,
  Inc.
15 West 16th St.
New York, NY 10011
(800) 232-5463
The Center has three components: National Technology Database, Evaluations, and Research and Development. It provides a resource for blind and visually impaired persons and professionals who work with them.

Northern Indiana Computer Education Lab (NICEL)

NICEL Lab
Indiana University at South Bend
South Bend, IN 46634
(219) 237-4352

The NICEL Lab is an instruction, preview, evaluation, and demonstration center for special educators in Indiana. The lab provides consultation on the implementation of technology in educational systems and maintains a database of evaluated software applicable for special education.

Psychological Software and Resources
Joseph C. Clancy, Ed.D.
97 Manchester Rd.
Newton Highlands, MA 02161
(617) 969-2614

Over 150 psychological software programs and resources, the database includes resources in the areas of cognitive skill practice, IEP goals and objectives, statistical packages, turnkey systems, memory skills, automated administration, and test scoring. The database also contains information on hotlines and 800 telephone number information resources.

REHABDATA Subscription Service
National Rehabilitation Information Center
8455 Colesville Rd.
Suite 935
Silver Spring, MD 20910-3319
(800) 346-2742

The REHABDATA bibliograpic database can be purchased in machine-readable versions. Subscribers may choose to purchase the entire database containing approximately 24,000 records of research reports, scholarly papers, policy papers, annual reports, progress reports, final reports, monographs, conference proceedings, journal articles, audiovisuals and reference works.

Rural Rehabilitation Technologies Database
University of North Dakota
Medical Center, Rehabilitation Hospital
Grand Forks, ND 58202
(701) 780-2489

This organization maintains a database containing information about technological devices of interest to disabled people.

The Sensory Technology Information Service
University Center on Aging
University of Massachusetts Medical Center
Worcester, MA 01655
(617) 856-6506

STIS provides comprehensive, up-to-date information on available technology and special services for individuals of all ages with hearing and vision impairments. STIS has over 2500 products on its database, in addition to other resources including consultants, literature, vendor contacts, and other databases.

Software to Go
Gallaudet University
800 Florida Ave., NE
Washington, DC 20002
(202) 651-5705

Software to Go is an information clearinghouse and lending library of microcomputer software for schools and programs concerned with the education of deaf students. Any school or educational program serv-

ing deaf or hard of hearing learners
is eligible to participate. Information
regarding microcomputer software
may be requested either by title or
subject. Software reviews are solic-
ited from educators of the deaf and
entered into the Software to Go
database. Software may be borrowed
for hands-on examination.

SOLUTIONS
Apple Computer, Inc.
20525 Mariani Ave., MS 2SE
Cupertino, CA 95014
(408) 974-7910, (408) 974-7911 (TDD)
   Apple's Worldwide Disability
Solutions Group communicates
regularly with nearly every
manufacturer and organization that
produces technology products and
related information of importance to
individuals with disabilities. The
results are organized in a comprehensive database that describes
more than a thousand adaptive
devices, software programs, and
disability-related organizations,
publications, and networks. SOLU-
TIONS is available on AppleLink,
SpecialNet and in the form of a
HyperCard stack.

**Special Needs Technology Data-
   base on Disk**
Tell 'em Ware
1714 Olson Way
Marshalltown, IA 50518
(515) 752-9667
   Tell 'em Ware offers an Apple-
Works database of information on
organizations, institutions and individuals who offer information or
services related to special needs technology.

Specialware Database
LINC Resources, Inc.
Publications Division
91 Vine St.
Pawtucket, RI 02861
(401) 725-3973
   The Specialware database contains nearly 800 descriptions of software programs for special education.
It is available in a variety of electronic and print formats. The software programs cover the full spectrum of special education, from early
childhood to adult education, mildly
handicapped to severely handicapped, reading to word processing
to administration. The database will
be updated on a regular basis.

Appendix I:
Toll-Free
Telephone Services

ABLEDATA (800) 344-5405

American Council of the Blind (800) 424-8666

American Foundation for the Blind (800) 232-5463

American Speech-Language-Hearing Association (800) 638-8255

Architectural and Transporation Barriers Compliance Board (800) 872-2253

Association for Retarded Citizens (800) 433-5255

Association of Radio Reading Service, Inc. (800) 255-2777

Association on Mental Retardation (800) 424-3688

Center for Special Education Technology (800) 873-8255

Cystic Fibrosis Foundation (800) 344-4823

Epilepsy Foundation of America (Consumers) (800) 332-1000; (Professional Library) (800) 332-4050

Estate Planning for the Disabled (800) 448-1071

Family Survival Project (CA only) (800) 445-8106

Federal Student Aid Information Center (800) 433-3243

HEATH Resource Center (800) 544-3284

IBM National Support Center for Persons with Disabilities (Voice) (800) 426-2133; (TDD) (800) 284-9482

Job Accommodation Network (800) 526-7234

Job Opportunities for the Blind (800) 638-7518

Modern Talking Picture Services, Inc. (800) 237-6213

National AIDS Information Clearinghouse (800) 342-2437; Spanish (800) 344-7432; (TDD) (800) 243-7889

National Alliance for the Mentally Ill (800) 950-6264

National Alliance of Blind Students (800) 424-8666

National Captioning Institute, Inc. (Voice) (800) 533-9673; (TDD) (800) 321-8337

National Center for Youth with Disabilities (800) 333-6293

National Committee for Citizens in Education (800) 638-9675

National Down Syndrome Congress (800) 232-6372

National Head Injury Foundation (800) 444-6443

National Health Information Center (800) 336-4797

National Information Center for Children and Youth with Disabilities (800) 999-5599

National Organization for Rare Disorders, Inc. (800) 999-6673

National Rehabilitation Information Center (800) 346-2742

National Spinal Cord Injury Association (800) 962-9629

Orton Dyslexia Society (800) 222-3123

Parent Educational Advocacy Training Center (800) 869-6782

Peterson's Guides (800) 388-3282

Recording for the Blind, Inc. (Book Orders Only) (800) 221-4792

Social Security Administration (800) 234-5772, (TDD) (800) 325-0778

Spina Bifida Association of America (800) 621-3141

Spinal Cord Injury Hotline (American Paralysis Assn.) (800) 526-3456

United Cerebral Palsy Associations (800) 872-1827

Woodbine House (800) 843-7323

Index to the Text